Bob Hope

PETER CARRICK

ROBERT HALE · LONDON

© *Peter Carrick 1988, 2003*
First published in Great Britain 1988
Reprinted in paperback with changes 2003

ISBN 0 7090 7299 6

Robert Hale Limited
Clerkenwell House
Clerkenwell Green
London EC1R 0HT

The right of Peter Carrick to be identified as
author of this work has been asserted by him
in accordance with the Copyright, Design and
Patents Act 1988

A catalogue record for this book is available from the British Library

Printed and bound in Malta by
Gutenberg Press Limited, Tarxien

Contents

List of Illustrations

Picture credits

The National Film Archive: 2–4, 7–11, 13, 14, 19, 20; *Hitchin Comet*: 5; Len Blakey, *Hertfordshire Express*: 6; Popperfoto: 12, 16, 21–4, 26–8, 30–2, 35–40; Frank Symons: 17, 18, 25; Dick Smith, *Hitchin Gazette*: 29, 33; Bill Smith, *Hitchin Gazette*: 34; Alan Millard: 41.

Acknowledgements

This book would not have been written without the help and co-operation of many people. I particularly want to thank Ian Rogerson, who gave me the idea of a biography of Bob Hope, Alan Millard, and Bob's British cousin, Frank Symons, who patiently answered my questions and generously provided me with numerous records and documents. I am also particularly indebted to Maria Francis and Elaine Stephenson for all their help, and to Ted Long, Jon Gornall, Peter Cliffe, Barry Edwards, Rupert Gurney, David Boyce, Sheena Atkinson, Jacqueline Scott, Julie Brewer and Arthur Cresswell.

My special thanks are extended to the Beverley Sisters, Bob Monkhouse and Shirley Eaton, for spending time talking to me about their links with Bob Hope, and to Malcolm Campbell (*Golf Monthly*), Peter Haslam (*Golf World*), and Bill Robertson (*Golf Illustrated*) for their full and frank comments.

For permission to reproduce extracts from published material I am grateful to A.M. Heath and Robert Faith (*Bob Hope — A Life in Comedy* by Robert Faith), W.H. Allen (*The Road to Hollywood* by Bob Hope and Bob Thomas), Thames Methuen (*The Road to Eltham* by Charles Thompson), Robson Books (*My Side of the Road* by Dorothy Lamour, as told to Dick McInnes), Stanley Paul (*Confessions of a Hooker* by Bob Hope with Dwayne Netland), Columbus Books (*The Amazing Careers of Bob Hope* by Joe Morella, Edward Z. Epstein and Eleanor Clark), and Hamlyn Publishing Group (*History of Movie Comedy* by Janice Anderson).

Important sources of reference, in addition to the titles already mentioned, were *The Paramount Story* by John Douglas Eames (Octopus Books), *The United Artists Story* by Ronald Bergan (Octopus Books), *The MGM Story* by John Douglas Eames (Octopus Books and Sundial), *The Illustrated Encyclopaedia of the World's Great Movie Stars* by Ken Wlaschin (Salamander Books); *The Great Movie Stars* by David Shipman (Angus and

Robertson), *The Movie* (Orbis), *Star Billing* by David Brown (Futura), *Five Women I Love* by Bob Hope (Robert Hale), the Hertfordshire Library Service (Letchworth Garden City branch), The Letchworth Shop, Letchworth Garden City Heritage Museum, the Raymond Mander and Joe Mitchenson Theatre Collections, the North Herts Gazette Group and the *Herts Pictorial* (now *The Comet*), the National Film Institute Information Library, *The Washington Star, Time Magazine, The Cleveland Press,* Ohio, *The American Weekly, The Examiner, TV Times, Today, Daily Mail* and *Daily Express, Daily Telegraph* and the *Telegraph Sunday Magazine.*

1 The Road to America

Aside from being for many people the world's funniest man, with wealth almost beyond belief and a remarkable distinction which gives him a unique kind of 'nodding relationship' with royalty and heads of state, Bob Hope has never lost the common touch, nor his near obsessional interest in his roots. An American national now for more than eighty years, until a few years ago he frequently set aside the shirtsleeves comfort of California for the stolid greyness of Britain. His pilgrimages to relatives in north Hertfordshire became such a local legend that everyone there remains puzzled that *The Road To Hitchin* never figured in the phenomenally successful film series, in company with Bing Crosby and Dorothy Lamour, which established him as one of Hollywood's greatest funny men.

Despite the shattering difference in life-style, Bob fitted into the modest three-bedroomed semi-detached house of cousin Frank Symons in Brampton Park Road, Hitchin, with remarkable ease. 'When he arrives it is almost as if he has never been away,' said Frank some years ago. 'He takes us as we are, enjoys his cup of tea, likes to meet as many of his relatives as he can, and is relaxing to be with.' Frank's wife, Kathleen, who died in May 1987, said: 'He even makes us feel at home in our own house!' And when he steps out into the colourful and well-kept back garden and says, 'I love the English countryside ... isn't it beautiful in Frank's garden?', there is no mistaking the genuine sentiment in the remark.

In 1969 Bob turned down an invitation to visit Monte Carlo, preferring to spend the weekend with his Hitchin relatives. A year later a casual passer-by might have rubbed his eyes in disbelief at the sight of the world-famous comedian playing a round of golf with a few locals at nearby Letchworth Garden City Golf Club. This unlikeliest of occasions had been prompted one Saturday morning by a telephone call to the local *Citizen* newspaper office where the then editor, Ted Long, was putting in some extra time. 'Do you want a game of golf this afternoon?' enquired Ted's son at the other end of the line. Ted wasn't very keen but asked who wanted to know. 'Bob Hope,' said the lad. It was all the incentive Ted needed.

Bob, staying at London's Savoy Hotel, had been keen to fit in a round of golf before going on to visit his relatives in Hitchin. Said Ted Long: 'I had met him before when he had visited Hitchin and told him then that when next he was coming to north Herts and fancied a game of golf to let me know and I would arrange something.' A return call to the Savoy confirmed arrangements, and Bob and his PR man, Bobbie Bixler, arrived just before 4 pm. For Bob's sake Ted had kept the comedian's visit a secret and the clubhouse was virtually deserted, though Ted had roped in club secretary Frank Bird, who admittedly didn't take much persuading.

An enjoyable four-ball game over nine holes eventually ended with Bob shaping up for a five-foot putt to halve the hole and save the match. By now word had got about that Bob was in town and there was a ring of enthusiastic spectators round that final hole. With that characteristic angling of the head and familiar half smile, he first called out good-humouredly for someone to go and kill a dog which was barking in the distance, before calmly stroking the ball in. While Bixler played on to complete the eighteen holes, Bob returned to the Letchworth clubhouse, where there were now many people. He chatted amiably, signed autographs, met club captain Rupert Gurney, and added a name which to this day remains for many the most famous signature in the Letchworth Garden City Golf Club visitors' book.

Off-stage Bob is not a joke-a-minute bore, claims Frank Symons, but you're left in no doubt that an impish residual humour lurks perpetually just below the surface.

On another occasion when the famous comedian was enjoying being holed up in Frank's tiny house in Hitchin, local milkman Ray Wingate called for his week's money. With such a famous visitor in the house for only a short time, Frank impatiently asked Ray if he could 'leave it for now' as he had Bob Hope visiting. Ray had been handed some intriguing and enterprising excuses by customers wanting to put off paying their milk bill, but this was by far the most remarkable and ingenious, and he was about to say as much — when the great man himself appeared at the door. Full marks to milkman Ray: he'd be happy to delay payment if Bob would have a picture taken with him and his fellow milkman and brother Charles, standing by the Letchworth, Hitchin & District Co-operative Society milkfloat parked outside. Bob was happy to comply.

That incident happened on one of Bob's earlier visits to Britain, but the story didn't come to light until 1970 when Eamonn Andrews sprang the inevitable surprise on the comedian by opening his famous *This is Your Life* book. It was fitting that so many of his British relatives were invited to take part in the tribute, along with such international personalities as Lord Louis Mountbatten and singer Tony Bennett, for given any say in the matter, it would have been just as Bob himself would have wanted it.

Bob left Britain for the United States as a four-year-old in 1908 and returned for the first time in 1939, just three weeks before the outbreak of the Second World War. Even then he was reputed to be earning the almost unbelievable sum of £1,000 a week from his radio and film work, though his fortune-making *Road* films were yet to come. He was drawn to Hitchin because his grandfather, James Hope, lived there, then a sprightly ninety-six years of age. Bob had enormous affection and respect for the old man, who had been something of a party entertainer himself in earlier days. 'He taught me the comics' business,' said Bob. 'He was a great character and at ninety-five was still riding his bicycle round the Hertfordshire lanes. He was always the star turn at any party — a very witty guy, full of cracks.'

Bob was thrilled to spend time with his grandfather in the house James himself had built in Hitchin's Bearton Road, for the old man still retained a mischievous twinkle in his eyes almost to the day of his death just a month before his hundredth birthday. The affection was mutual, and James Hope was proud of his grandson. When for the first time he heard that Bob was to visit him for tea, he scoured Hitchin shops looking for a flag with 'Stars and Stripes' on. He proclaimed: 'My grandson, my young Bob, is coming to see me all the way from America. I must have the Stars and Stripes to welcome the lad.'

On this visit Bob joined about forty of his relatives in a local hotel to celebrate James' ninety-sixth birthday. Grandfather ran the show as MC, joked and sang 'My Lancashire Lass' among a number of songs, while Bob responded with an impromptu 'Smoke Gets in Your Eyes' in duet with his new wife, Dolores Reade, and offered an enthusiastically applauded demonstration of tap dancing in his inimitable labour-saving style.

Despite Bob's fame, Grandpa took control, having earlier taken Bob aside with: 'Now you leave this to me. I know these people.' Bob did, and said later: 'He was terrific. More jokes than I could think up in a week.' But Bob also owes something to his late mother, who as Avis Towns had been a concert singer in Wales. He acknowledges: 'I learned a lot about timing from her.'

Bob met his grandfather just once more, almost four years on, when he was back in Britain entertaining at military camps just before D-Day. His cousin, Frank Symons, said that he got a message from Bob, who was appearing at a military base not far away, asking if he could get Grandpa over to see him. 'I took him over and, after Bob spotted us in the audience, Grandfather was called up on stage. He said he was glad to see the American troops, wished them well for the forthcoming invasion and then, in typical style, said: "But it's taken you long enough to get over here," a reference to America's late entry into the war.' A short time after, Bob received word that the old man had died and insisted on being present at his funeral.

Bob will tell you with pride that Grandfather Hope had been a master stone-carver and had worked on the Royal Courts of Justice in the Strand in London and on repairs to St Paul's Cathedral. Around the mid-1800s, old man Hope formed a partnership with a friend called Percy Picton and set up business as builders in Hitchin. The firm built numerous houses in the town and also had the distinction of building some of the first dwellings in nearby Letchworth, shortly after its selection by social reformer Ebenezer Howard as the site for the world's first 'garden city'. The firm collected second prize there in a special competition for new homes. Hard times later forced the partnership out of business, but a number of Picton and Hope-built houses remain today in both towns, and the Picton side of the business still operates from nearby Knebworth.

It is endearing that an entertainer of such international stature, who is undoubtedly one of the richest men in America, should hold on so affectionately and steadfastly to his family links in all their comparative modesty. Bob used to enjoy nothing more than parking his shining black Rolls-Royce in the grey streets of Hitchin and having Sunday afternoon tea with his then eighty-year-old Aunt Lucy. On one occasion, unsure of the exact location of the house, he had his chauffeur park the limousine and was found by a local reporter wandering around trying to pin-point the house.

Standing in the beautifully tended back garden of Frank Symons' house, ludicrously diminutive compared with the lush acres of his own $10 million Space Age home in Palm Springs (which includes a fireplace bigger than Frank's living-room), he is not in the least condescending. He tells Frank his garden is a delight and really means it; and for the short time he is able to spare to be there, his whole bearing suggests that he wouldn't rather be anywhere else in the world.

Bob had no need to take the road to Hitchin as he did: everyone would have understood, even Frank Symons, if he couldn't find the time or lost the inclination to keep in touch. But even during his arduous overseas tours entertaining American troops in Vietnam and elsewhere over Christmas, his relatives weren't forgotten. For years Bob didn't spend Christmas at home and, although this meant that Frank Symons didn't get his Christmas card until January, it always turned up. Frank's late wife Kathleen told me: 'He never acts the big star. He appears to get his biggest joy out of seeing us.'

In the 1970s Bob had people in Britain look into his ancestry, searching for birth certificates and marriage licences at Somerset House and in obscure parish records. In all things concerning his family background in Britain he has always had an unquenchable interest. It is perhaps uncommon that he is so fascinated by his roots, but Frank Symons thinks that anyone who knows Bob well would not think it at all unusual. 'He is a man of very wide interests and gets absorbed in all sorts of things. He is proud of his British ancestry and, knowing him as I do, I don't consider it at all odd or unusual that he should be so interested in his family tree.'

Bob himself offers no serious explanation, except that he enjoys keeping in touch with his relatives. Certainly the reason he put forward to Her Majesty The Queen and a distinguished audience at a Royal Variety Show at the London Palladium in 1967 cannot be taken too seriously: 'I have to keep well in with my Hitchin relatives,' he proclaimed from the famous stage. 'I don't want to be left out of their will.'

Bob is known as an Anglo-Saxon institution, a staunch Anglophile, and he has been dragging friends and family over to Britain since the days when it took almost a week to make the trip from New York to Southampton by boat. Offhand he cannot remember how many times he has been to Britain, but his affection for the old country is genuine enough and even well into his eighties, he continued to make the effort to make the trip. He is obviously proud of his British background, loves the British and their capacity for understatement, and delights in the cosiness and greenery of the countryside.

Bob Hope was born at Eltham, near Lewisham in Kent on 29 May, 1903 and was christened Leslie Towns Hope. The first name came from a local soccer hero of the day, and Towns was his mother's family name. Avis Towns was a resourceful lady, the daughter of a Welsh seafarer, small but positive and forward-looking.

Bob's arrival, though welcomed with affection, cannot have been of momentous consequence. Large families were usual then, and his mother had already experienced five successful pregnancies. All were boys, all born in Britain; her seventh, yet to be born, would be the only one to be American by birthright. An only daughter, Emily, died as an infant.

Had baby Leslie's long-term future been contemplated at all, it might have been assumed that he would follow his father into building. William Henry Hope was a master stonemason and expert at the job, and for a time the Hope family were comfortably off. But as brick began rapidly to replace stone as the fashionable building material, Bob's father's undoubted talent became less commercial. Never one to put much aside for a rainy day, William Henry began filling his empty hours convivially in the local pubs and, increasingly, gambling on gaining a new pot of gold betting on the horses. A move from Eltham to Bristol did little to improve the family fortunes, and savings dwindled.

The world's most famous funny man might not have become an entertainer had his father been more sober, thrifty and fortunate. As it was, William Henry's increased drinking and gambling caused mounting friction at home until, with little prospect of work in Britain, he sank his last draught of British ale, said goodbye to his family and set off for America, where he joined his brothers Fred and Frank who were already established with their families in Cleveland, Ohio. He promised to send for his wife and children once he had gathered enough money together.

It was a gamble, but it worked. Hope found a demand for his skills in the United States. He worked hard and long and to such purpose that in March 1908, little more than eighteen months after he set out on his speculative trip, Avis Hope and their six sons arrived in New York after a turbulent Atlantic crossing, steerage class. Before finding a house of their own, the Hopes lived with various aunts, uncles and cousins in Cleveland, but soon Avis found a home for them, and young Leslie attended school for the first time.

Though Bob remembers both his mother and father with affection, these were not the best days of his life. His father never adapted to the American way of life, and as his opportunities and disposition for regular work dwindled, his drinking once again increased and he became more distant from his family. It was left to Bob's mother to hold the family together, and she and the boys became very close. She set the standards, provided courage and purpose when most needed and, perhaps above all, showed by example and inspiration the value of optimism and determination.

Avis also sang as she went about the house. Having been a concert singer in her younger days, music was important to her. Even when the family budget was low, she insisted on buying a second-hand piano.

Bob also acknowledges his father's influence: 'When he was in the mood, he would entertain us for hours with jokes and tales.' Given that background, it is hardly surprising that Bob should turn naturally to singing and entertaining when he wanted to earn himself pocket money a few years later. It was usual for high-school kids to run errands and take on all manner of chores to earn extra money. In Bob's case, with family finances hard pressed, the only pocket money he would get was what he earned.

He told Charles Thompson in *The Road from Eltham:* 'It just seemed natural that I should sing, so when Sunday rolled around, and we were broke, a bunch of us would board a street-car for Luna Park [the local amusement park] and begin singing popular songs. I'd sing solo. Then we'd give out with a quartet. Then, just before getting to Luna, we'd pass the hat and split the proceeds.' Though some of the earnings were spent at the park, street-corner singing on the way home would net a few more dollars which would go into the family fund. He would also pick up extra coppers playing pool at the billiard halls. At one point, the amount of time he was spending in the halls caused concern, but his mother had an intuitive feeling about her son's future, and insisted he would make out.

The cinema was Bob's passion; Rudolph Valentino and later Charles Chaplin were his idols. He spent a lot of time at the movies, his visits financed by a succession of part-time jobs, which included selling newspapers, working in his eldest brother's butcher's shop and delivering bread.

Making extra cash to help out was a family affair. Bob's mother had earlier started to take in boarders, and they moved house a couple of times to give expanded opportunities. Avis Hope was a tower of strength. She encouraged and directed, set good standards, loved her children dearly and earned their respect and affection. Bob was reasonably athletic at school. He could use his fists and ran well. The summer weekend parties organized by the big firms in Cleveland for their employees generally included races, and Bob was often among the winners, competing in as many as three picnic events in a day where prizes could be as high as $5.

But as time went on, it was the movies which captured more of his attention and interest. Bob looked to the time when he might become another Charlie Chaplin and in the meantime dressed up like the great comic to win one of the Chaplin look-alike contests which were popular at that time. Though bright, he was far less captivated by the academic side of school life and at the first opportunity left to make his way in the world.

At fifteen, the First World War just ended, a job was a job, and Bob tried his hand at quite a number. He reckons he lost his first job as a night-shift parts clerk in the Chandler Motor Company's Cleveland car plant through singing into the office dictaphone machine as one of an impromptu vocal quartet. Explaining his dismissal in one of his books, Bob said: 'One morning the boss came in and pushed the button. We'd forgotten to erase the song.' Journalism and pugilism fleetingly seized his attention, but instinctively he seemed drawn towards show business. The tap lessons he had taken while at school from King Rastus Brown, a black entertainer of the day, and his success in earlier amateur shows provided the impetus for his first gentle nudge towards a stage career.

Bob now enrolled with former vaudeville performer Johnny Root at his local dance school. After only six months and with the school faltering financially, he stepped in and took it over. He had business cards printed: 'Leslie T. Hope will teach you how to dance', and set about saving the school. It was a lost cause. Though he managed to keep things going for a while, his dream of prospering from running his own dance academy dissolved as the bankrupt school finally had to put up the shutters.

Among Bob's youthful heroes were comedians Roscoe Arbuckle and Harry Langdon, and curiously both were later to figure importantly in his life, the former in pointing him on the road to a professional career on stage, the latter in offering a valuable lesson for life. But in the meantime, at nineteen and with a keen eye for the opposite sex, Leslie Towns Hope managed to persuade his current girlfriend, Mildred Rosequist, to join him as a dance partner. As a semi-pro team with limited ambition, they did well in local shows in and around their hometown. Bob applied himself well and made up quite a structured dance act but soon became dissatisfied at earning only $8 for a Saturday night performance. He was ready to make a bold bid for fame outside Cleveland. Although Mildred might have been tempted, her parents didn't share Bob's enthusiasm for having their daughter venture to more distant venues, remaining away from home with him for weeks and maybe months on end. When the promising partnership split up, Bob teamed with an old friend, Lloyd Durbin, working up an act which, after winning a fair local reputation, was able to go out on the road.

A year to remember for Bob Hope was 1924, the venue the Bandbox Theatre in Cleveland. The manager there had booked in as featured attraction the famous comedian Roscoe 'Fatty' Arbuckle. Although already past his most famous days, he was nevertheless a big name and expensive to book for a small, struggling theatre like the Bandbox. 'Fatty' Arbuckle is still remembered in show business. Born in 1887, he learned the trade coming up the hard way in American vaudeville before going into films where, as an extra, his comedy potential was cleverly spotted by Mack Sennett, who masterminded the fabulous success of the Keystone Kops. Under Sennett's guidance Arbuckle became probably the greatest slapstick comedian of his time, appearing in numerous silent movies. Always happy to poke fun at his own ample proportions in the cause of film comedy, he also became the king of the custard pie, reputably able to throw two at a time, one with each hand, with uncanny accuracy.

Arbuckle was as great in his own way as Chaplin and Buster Keaton were in theirs. At one point he was said to be earning $1,000 a day and in 1921 was given a three-year contract worth $3 million.

But that same year his career ended disastrously and almost overnight. He was the centre of a notorious Hollywood scandal involving a young starlet called Virginia Rappe, who died tragically at a wild party. Although Arbuckle was eventually cleared by jury of her death by 'rape or some other means', Hollywood film-makers were in no position to forget, as the public turned against him. His films were banned, he was barred from making or directing films, and he finally died of a heart attack in 1933 when only 46.

When Bob Hope appeared on the same bill with him at the Bandbox, Arbuckle was still very much a hero to the young man. Hope and Durbin performed well at the Bandbox, fitting into their tightly organized act a tap dance, a soft-shoe routine, the song 'Sweet Georgia Brown' and a kind of pantomime Egyptian comedy number.

Arbuckle, somewhat pathetically attempting a stage comeback after the Hollywood scandal, was impressed by their act and promised to recommend them to a prominent producer of small touring revues called Fred Hurley. He was as good as his word, and Bob and his partner were hired for a show called *Hurley's Jolly Follies*.

Bob never forgot 'Fatty' Arbuckle's kindness, nor the advice given to him some time later by another comedy star of silent films who, curiously enough, also ended his career disastrously. Baby-faced star Harry Langdon once told Bob: 'If you ever go out to Hollywood and become a star, don't make my mistake. Don't try to convince yourself that you're a genius.' Langdon, more than most, had cause to utter the words.

The genius behind his success was film director Frank Capra, who in those days was gag-writing for Langdon. Such was their success together that in the 1920s Warner Brothers offered Harry Langdon $6,000 a week to work for them, and he accepted, shrewdly taking Capra along with him. After further enormous successes together, when Langdon decided he was now such a big star that he could make his own films, he summarily sacked Capra. The films he made himself were abject failures, his career plummeted, and eventually he was glad to accept supporting roles. He was still trying to make a comeback when he died a bankrupt in 1944. Said Bob later: 'I always remembered Harry's words and never made his mistake in believing that movies are a do-it-yourself project.' It was Harry Langdon who made Bob realize that movie-making is a collaborative effort and, because of what Harry said, Bob always tried to place himself in the hands of the best creative minds and the best technicians.

By now Hope and Durbin were earning $40 a week on the Fred Hurley circuit and seemed content with that. Then the partnership ended abruptly when Lloyd Durbin was suddenly taken ill with food poisoning and died.

In those days vaudeville was a hard, tiring business. It was locked in a death struggle, fighting the combined onslaught of a powerfully developing radio and an even more powerful film business, now with the added potency of sound. Touring companies travelled in battered coaches and stayed in cheap rooming-houses. On stage you had to be capable of turning your hand to almost anything, and Bob used to sing, joke, dance, act, even play an instrument. It was gruelling and poorly paid but an effective grounding and a rewarding experience. Despite the discomfort of the life and the instability, Bob looked upon it as an inevitable step on the road to success and recognition.

After Lloyd Durbin's death, he teamed with dancer George Byrne, and they put together a competent act which concentrated more on straight comedy. Their first major move up from the bottom rung of vaudeville came when they presented a straight comedy revue called *The Blackface Follies,* for which they blacked up their faces and appeared at McKeesport in Pennsylvania. They were such novices at the business that they used black greasepaint instead of burnt cork and had the rest of the troupe holding their sides as they spent hours scrubbing off the greasepaint at the end of the show. By 1926 they were earning $50 a week, with Bob as the stooge and George the comedian.

A year later the act said farewell to Fred Hurley, to grab the offer of an engagement to appear in Detroit for $225 a week. Other bookings in the Detroit area followed, then a $300 a week stint in Pittsburgh, after which Hope and Byrne felt confident the time was right to take New York by storm.

With no forward bookings, they found New York unfriendly, uncharitable and rock hard when it came to finding engagements. After scores of auditions and a few one-night stands in seedy theatres best forgotten, they managed to get a booking with the Keith & Orpheus Circuit. Convinced they were on the verge of better days, they devised a new, highly complicated act which included a slapstick dance routine involving firemen's helmets, hose pipes and water being sloshed around the stage. It was hardly the sort of act on which big-time careers are based, and soon their long-cherished Broadway début seemed farther away than ever. Cash reserves dwindled, they skimped on food and accommodation, and Bob's bodyweight dropped worryingly. At one time they each convinced the other, if not themselves, that it was time to quit and go home.

At the moment of their greatest despair, show business played its most cruel blow, sending their spirits soaring, only to drag them down soon afterwards. They were cast on Broadway in a promising production of *The Sidewalks of New York* which received good reviews and enjoyed a long run. Sadly, when they might reasonably have expected to be on the verge of the big time, the small song-and-dance number in which they featured with the talented Ruby Keeler (then a virtually unknown chorus girl and dancer but later to gain fame in those outrageous Busby Berkeley musicals) was hammered by the critics and taken out of the show.

2   Friends Along the Way

Cinema idols from the golden age of the movies often served long and uncomfortable apprenticeships on stage. When Bob Hope was unceremoniously booted out of the cast of *The Sidewalks of New York,* he was already a vaudeville veteran of five long and uncharitable years. Although he was given a screen test only three years later, in 1930, it was not for another eight years that his first Hollywood feature film was released.

Being axed from their first Broadway show was a hard lesson for Hope and Byrne, but indirectly it signalled the end of the partnership and a sharpening of Hope's potential as a stand-up comedian. Having at last reached Broadway, however fleetingly, they shunned the idea of turning back. In 1927 Broadway had not yet wilted before the massive onslaught of a swiftly emerging film industry (boosted that very year by the coming of sound) and Hope and Byrne remained there. They achieved little, however, and eventually heeded the advice of astute Johnny Hyde, of the William Morris Agency, to move out and start again with a fresh act. Bob made contact with Cleveland agent Mike Shea, who booked them into an insignificant venue at New Castle in Pennsylvania, at just $50 gross for three days work. It was a humbling experience after the bright lights of Broadway, but with only three acts appearing on the bill, Hope and Byrne were able to claim a featured slot as the 'stars' appearing at the end of the programme.

Their act hardly pulled the house down. What was significant, however, was the manager's idea of asking Bob to announce the forthcoming attractions at the end of the show. Bob included a joke or two, and the audience liked it much more than his fooling and dancing with George Byrne. His now legendary quip about a Scotsman on the following week's bill who got married in the backyard, so the chickens could get the rice, was enthusiastically applauded. The manager was so impressed that for the next performance he made sure that Bob was given more time. The audience again loved it, giving Bob a great reception in his new stand-up comic role. When someone afterwards suggested that he pack up the double act and concentrate on being a master of ceremonies, he and Byrne talked seriously about the future for the first time.

Perhaps intuitively Bob had been slowly moving towards a split in the partnership, though in their earlier days together he had been the straight man while George Byrne took care of the funny lines. They had set out two years before with an adventurous spirit and a rugged determination to make it to the top, and having made Broadway, however briefly, was certainly no mean feat. Even so, they agreed that the act didn't seem to have much future. Byrne was older than Bob, and the grind of starting again almost from scratch didn't appeal. Bob's success on his own was all Byrne needed to convince him that it was time for him to retire. The break was made in an amicable spirit.

With Byrne gone, Bob was left with a routine not substantially dissimilar from some of his earlier offerings. He 'blacked up' and, in a costume which included cotton gloves and a big red bow tie, cracked jokes, finishing with a song and dance. The blackened face was abandoned when, arriving late one night at the theatre, he had no time to apply the make-up and went on stage without it — and drew more applause! Said Bob years later: 'Mike Shea told me my face was funnier the way it was.'

Bookings were brisk in and around his hometown of Cleveland. Billed as 'Leslie T. Hope', he did the circuit of one-nighters and, although the money wasn't exciting, at least it was regular. Relatively it was also secure, for Mike Shea had plenty of dates lined up. But Bob's ambition towered above the tedious round of hometown engagements and before long, ignoring Shea's advice to stay put, he headed west for Chicago, on what he hoped would be the first leg of a return to the bright lights of Broadway.

In Chicago he was unknown and unwanted. He failed to secure even one booking. In debt and in some desperation, he changed his name to Lester T. Hope: '. . . it was a little more mannish and could not be confused with a girl's name,' he explained. The switch signalled a change of luck, for an old school friend, Charlie Cooley, introduced him to booking agent

Charlie Hogan, who managed to get Bob a three-day engagement at the West Englewood Theatre. At $25 for each performance, it was hardly the big time, but it turned out to be significant, leading to a booking at the Chicago Stratford Theatre.

It was customary then for theatres to change programmes each week, but to have a permanent MC who would link the individual acts with a few jokes and a song. The Stratford's MC had become very popular, particularly with the regular patrons, but had also become difficult to work with, which led to his dismissal. Bob filled the gap with such success that his original engagement was extended to two weeks and he was to stay at the Stratford for six months, being paid $300 a week, the most he had ever earned.

Bob Hope's career only broadly followed the traditional pattern. He didn't achieve worldwide fame with an overnight blockbuster. Nor did he make it in one specific medium. Similarly, his stage career did not take a steady course, progressing step by step to top billing on Broadway. It could be argued indeed that he enjoyed only a flash of Broadway stardom before moving into films and, up to that point, might many times have given up altogether, such was the erratic nature of his career.

At the Stratford he seemed poised for bigger and better things, but the need to find a constant supply of new material became too stressful. Theatre-going was popular, and it was not unusual for people to visit the same theatre a couple of times a week. Even the best joke was dead after the first telling, and Bob, in these days before professional gag-writers, gave up the incessant search for fresh humour. He decided to form a new partnership with Louise Troxell, his girlfriend at that time, in an act which toured the western vaudeville circuit.

As they faced a procession of dates in small towns in America's Midwest, this shift in his career could scarcely be considered progress. Indeed, at Fort Worth, Texas, some time later, while working Bob O'Donnell's Interstate Time Circuit, Bob's rapid-fire joking hardly raised a laugh among the slow-talking locals. It was left to O'Donnell himself to teach Bob an important lesson — that no matter how good the material, it had to be professionally delivered, slowly enough for the audience to hear and appreciate, with emphasis and a fine sense of timing. He told Bob to slow down, to be less nervous and more relaxed and to time his delivery with a sensitivity to audience reaction. It was excellent advice which Bob worked on immediately, and once the Fort Worth audiences could hear him, they loved him.

But Texas fell well short of Broadway, and Bob was still fixed on reaching the top. In one major leap, and with the help and influence of Bob O'Donnell, he *almost* made it, for the biggest booking agency in American vaudeville, the B.F. Keith office, decided to take him on. In a sense it was an important breakthrough, in another a disappointment, for the deal put Hope and Troxell to the test, everything hinging on their ability to prove themselves at the Proctor, one of the group's less important theatres just off Broadway.

By this time Lester T. Hope had become Bob Hope — some were later to suggest that it was in acknowledgement of O'Donnell's help — but the name-change was no therapy for his immediate fears.

The Proctor was known for its tough audiences, so Bob decided to take a minor booking across the river in Brooklyn as a test-run for the act before the vital appearance there. It was a nightmare. Hope and Troxell were unable to make any kind of impact. They almost wrote off the Proctor opening in advance.

One element which was to be vital to Bob Hope's future worldwide success had its baptism during that very performance. Silent screen star John Gilbert's marriage antics were at that time making big news, and John's wife, the famous movie actress Leatrice Joy, had been the preceding act. Bob walked out on stage and without hesitation cracked two or three jokes about the star's domestic situation after first announcing, 'No, lady. . . this is not John Gilbert.' The audience roared approval, and the topical gag had found a new meaning.

Bob was to develop the technique over the years, often pushing the topical innuendo to the verge of unacceptable insolence, but never beyond. Others were to follow his example, but no one approached Hope's polished and well-calculated delivery, supreme sense of timing and inward innocence, so that the jibes and the jokes always fell short of offence. The way he delivered his material, the rapport he developed with his audience, the style and manner of his act, put him ahead of his contemporaries. He could virtually say what he liked; nobody was upset.

The Proctor success resulted in Hope and Troxell signing a contract worth $450 a week. But then again, when Bob seemed on the verge of Broadway success, he veered off course, this time tempted by the sunshine coastline of California and the Hollywood film studios of his childhood dreams. The West Coast liked the act and he and Louise played a number of useful dates before moving back to New York, where they were engaged for the revue *Antics of 1931* at the Palace Theatre.

Compared with thousands of victims of the Wall Street Crash, Bob Hope had been relatively unscathed by the Depression, but by this time radio and films were pushing hard into the public's consciousness and, faced also with major competition from close-by theatres, the famed Palace, still the Mecca for many vaudevillians, was losing money heavily. But after the first night's performance, Bob had other things to worry over; a biting criticism of his performance — which suggested that, as he had reputedly been a sensation in the American Midwest, he perhaps ought to go back there — had him on the verge of quitting on the spot. Bob credits first humorist Harry Hershfield and then established vaudevillians Ken Murray and Ted Healey with helping him over the trauma and into an established pattern of work which was to keep him in New York, with some isolated excursions outside, for about six years.

Broadway was one thing, but for a stand-up comic like Bob, still with some reputation to make, opportunities to appear in smash-hit Broadway shows were not on offer round every street corner. Vaudeville was still the bread-and-butter business, and Bob was proud to be part of it. In later years he was to look back with strong affection on this period of his career. 'I'll always remember my days in New York. They were great times,' he recalled.

Also, though he had played his first few rounds of golf back in 1927 on a public course in Cleveland, and failed miserably, it was during his years in New York that he developed his life-long obsession with the game.

Regular work brought its own fun and stimulus. Bob took his first exciting steps as a radio comedian on the eve of a decade when radio was all-powerful as a means of mass communication and entertainment. He also pioneered the new art of engaging gag-writers and, perhaps most important of all, as Bob himself will take pains to point out (handing you the information tightly wrapped up in the latest crack), it was while he was in New York that he met and partnered Dolores Reade, not only on stage but for life.

Professional critics had a powerful role in forming public opinion in the 1930s, and Bob had every reason to be haunted by his poor notices in *Antics of 1931*. Fortunately Billy Grady, who was at that time Al Jolson's manager, saw Bob's performance and was big enough to make up his own mind. Talking later with some key characters heavily involved in a forthcoming Broadway show, he recommended Hope to them. Bob was still under contract to the Keith office and, following the closing of *Antics of 1931*, had been busy for them on a number of vaudeville engagements, still with his established partner, Louise Troxell. The group wanted him for their new show, *Ballyhoo of 1932*, but sadly there was no spot for Louise. The Keith office gave permission, but disappointingly Bob's new opportunity meant a break-up of his partnership with Louise. Approaching thirty and having been treading the boards for close on ten years, he now became a recognized solo performer for the first time. At $600 a week, it was the most he had yet earned.

The show opened in September and closed just four months later; but for all that, *Ballyhoo of 1932* was crucial to the development of Bob's showbiz career for, by accident, it gave him the opportunity to project and exploit his uncanny natural feel for the ad-lib situation.

His instinctive gift to talk and joke himself out of any situation might well have taken longer to surface publicly had it not been for behind-the-scenes chaos before curtain-up on *Ballyhoo*'s out-of-town opening in Atlantic City. First-night nerves resulted in a communications breakdown backstage, delaying the opening. The situation grew desperate as the orchestra completed the overture, then started going through it again. The audience became impatient and restless. The famous Shubert brothers, among the most influential impresarios of the day, with a name for spotting and developing talent, had money in the show and, as the minutes ticked away, Lee Shubert in some desperation pushed Bob on stage with orders to entertain the audience until the show was ready to begin. With no time to resist, Bob found himself centre-stage, with an irritated audience to pacify and entertain.

It was usual then for 'warm-up' acts to open and close the programmes — tumblers, acrobats and similar neutral acts which acted as background for late arrivals and early leavers.

Bob's opening gambit struck home with his audience: 'Ladies and Gentlemen, this is the first time I've ever been on before the acrobats.' Then, for all of five minutes, he gave an impromptu recital of jokes, even at one point indirectly involving the audience. 'Hello, Sam,' he called out after peering up into the balcony. Then, in confidence to the audience: 'That's one of our backers up there. He says he's not nervous, but I notice that he buckled his safety belt.'

Bemused and uncertain at the start, the audience found Bob's act so convincing that they thought it a deliberate and novel introduction to the show. The disaster averted, Shubert showed his gratitude by insisting that Bob open the show in similar style on a regular basis. He resisted, unable to contemplate similar torture every night of the week. Mr Shubert persisted. In the end a deal was struck, with Bob performing a scripted routine called 'The Complaint Department' ahead of the overture, sitting in a made-up box resembling a store complaints desk. But even this couldn't save the ill-conceived, pedestrian show.

During this time Bob met Bing Crosby for the first time, on 42nd Street near the Friars Club in New York, popular with theatricals. There was no hint then that just two months later they would be working together.

Bob returned to the Keith organization after the failure of *Ballyhoo* and was booked into the Capitol Theatre as resident MC. When he looked at his advance list of acts appearing, he was astonished to find Bing's name on it. The singer was already a star, having featured with Paul Whiteman's band and then as one of the Rhythm Boys trio in his first movie, in 1930, called *King of Jazz*. Then in 1932, after a temporary eclipse, musical films became fashionable again and Paramount, eager to make money by fitting films round known radio and record stars, cast Bing in *The Big Broadcast*.

Said Bob many years later: 'He was extremely cordial to a peasant out of vaudeville. In fact we worked up some routines together to delight the Capitol audiences.' Bob went on to explain that one of the routines was an old vaudeville standby about two men meeting on the street.

Two Farmers: 'We approached each other from opposite sides of the stage, then I pointed my thumbs down and Bing milked them,' explained Bob.

Two Politicians: 'We hailed each other, then started picking each other's pockets.'

Tame by today's standards maybe, but in 1932 these and similar routines worked out by Bob and Bing had the Capitol audiences clamouring for more. Almost seven years later they re-ran some of them at a special performance to mark the opening of the new season at the Del Mar race track, then being operated by Bing and Pat O'Brien. Among the Hollywood guests was the production boss of Paramount Pictures, William LeBaron, who was so struck by the way Bob and Bing worked together that he got the idea of putting them in a movie as a comedy duo. The film to emerge was *Road to Singapore*, which also teamed the sultry Dorothy Lamour, already the undisputed queen of the South Sea island sarong.

It was during his New York days that Bob first met Dorothy. Living at 65 Central Park West, he was already into his life-long habit of taking a midnight stroll before turning in, and on one occasion he dropped into the One Fifth Avenue night club, where Dorothy was singing. Later she took a two-week engagement at the Club Navarre on Central Park South, a favourite spot for comedians, and Bob often showed up. He'd listen to her sing and have a chat, and on one occasion introduced her to his girlfriend, Dolores.

It is well known now that Bob and Dorothy found film fame together in the *Road* films, but not that Dotty was cast with Bob before that, in his first Hollywood movie, *The Big Broadcast of 1938*. In this Bob was very much on trial and, according to Dotty, Paramount were not at all certain that they would pick up his option once the picture was over. Bob's problem, said Dotty, was that Paramount felt he was too similar to the already well-established Jack Benny. In her autobiography, *My Side of the Road,* she reveals that she was so certain that Bob would become a major star, given the opportunity, that she even offered to let the studio cut her own salary and give one half to Bob. 'I told them if they would please take up his option and put him in a few pictures — the right ones — they would have another big star who some day would be an institution.' Later, when Bob amassed one of the biggest fortunes in Hollywood, the joke of her giving him half her salary was appreciated as keenly by Dotty as by Hope himself. 'When I said he would become an institution, I should have said a banking institution,' she joked.

Despite Dorothy Lamour's intervention on Bob's behalf, he

was fortunate to be given another chance by Paramount. *The Big Broadcast of 1938* was a mediocre offering, hauled out of its tedious and eccentric plot by the outstanding success of its featured song, 'Thanks for the Memory'. This melody, now something of a classic among pop standards because Bob was to adopt it as his theme, was sung by Bob and Shirley Ross in the film. It caught the attention of the public, who bought copies of the record in thousands, at a time when popular music was yet to become an industry. Moreover, the film made money for Paramount, who, with annual profits that year dropping uneasily below the $3 million mark against more than double that figure in 1936, were more than willing to be guided by the merry sound of the cash registers. They renewed Hope's contract.

It was while they were at the Capitol that Bob and Bing worked out the basic formula for their professional mock rivalry. In its developed form later in their individual careers it was to place no restriction on the number or extent of the insults and innuendos each would cast at the other. In a bar close to the Capitol Theatre they would often be seen scheming their stage routines. They got on well privately, and their natural off-stage good-natured banter was cleverly worked up for public benefit. It reflected to an almost uncanny degree their own casual, relaxed, easy-going personalities.

The act they put together for their short stay at the Capitol was only one step ahead of an average vaudeville turn, but it opened the door to the visual gagging to be found in the *Road* films. Bob would tell the audience that unfortunately his partner couldn't be with him because someone had locked him in the washroom. Bing would wander on from the other side of the stage holding a brass door-knob fixed to a chunk of splintered wood. Supposedly unaware of Bob's presence, he too would explain that his partner would not be with him that night because he had a stomach upset. Bob, striding forth indignantly, would retort that he certainly did not have an upset stomach. Brandishing the door-knob in front of Hope's face, Bing's wind-up line would bring the house down: 'You will after you swallow this.'

Against all the complex facets of humour in the 1980s, this example of early Hope-Crosby duelling is glaringly dated. At the time, though, it had a strong appeal and, stimulated by the increasing force of sound radio, would become snappier, cleverer, smoother and more sophisticated. Bob's work would always include cracks against Bing. Bing would try to get at Bob in his routines. Of course the *Road* films used props and visual eccentricities effectively, but as a solo comedian Bob would depend more and more on verbal skill, quality of material, timing and delivery to get his laughs at the expense of Crosby. Others were to copy the elements of scorn, ridicule and contempt which were the basis of this running relationship, but none would capture Bob's style, unpretentiousness and spontaneity. As a stand-up comic, Bob had greater opportunity than Bing to use the device, and the formula, worked out in its most rudimentary form at New York's Capitol Theatre all those years before, though refined and sophisticated over the years, became an automatic commitment whenever either was performing, to be destroyed only by Bing's shock death in 1977.

While Bing Crosby remained the prime target of Hope's insults and 'put down' one-liners, Bob developed the technique to the extreme, peppering his television, radio, stage and personal appearances with classic comedy lines about Jack Benny, Fred Allen, George Burns, Frank Sinatra and scores of others in public life. No one was safe: sportsmen and women, crooks and do-gooders, newspaper columnists, beauty queens, his own glamorous co-stars, anyone even temporarily in the headlines — all became candidates for the Hope treatment, to be identified specifically by name, even politicians, heads of state, religious leaders and royalty. The personal joke increasingly became the basis of his performance, but it was never calculated to offend.

Back in the 1930s radio made fast and dramatic progress. No longer was it dominated by music, and as it widened its horizons the pace quickened to haul in talent from all sides, with vaudeville an obvious hunting-ground and Bob a fair target. He made his radio début in the *Capitol Family Hour* and went on to appear in the weekly *Fleischman Hour* with Rudy Vallee. But he was back working in vaudeville, at the New York Palace on a bill being run in conjunction with the theatre's weekly film, when he was spotted by noted theatrical producer Max Gordon.

All the previous winter the celebrated composer Jerome Kern and talented lyricist Otto Harbach had been working on a new musical romance based on Alice Duer Miller's book *Gowns by Roberta*. Max Gordon had been brought in as producer after he and Kern, working as director for the first time, had been at loggerheads over misunderstandings concerning an earlier show.

The row flared again when Gordon wanted Hope for the part of the comic in their new show. Some sources say that Gordon later claimed that Kern had accused him of trying to palm him off with one of his old vaudevillians. On one point, it should be said in Kern's defence, there was no doubt: Bob was very much a late choice. Gordon admitted he had gone through all the obvious candidates without success before following up a lead and going to the Palace to see Bob perform. The role in the new show called for a comic of some experience who could handle the kind of fluent patter required of an MC, and Bob, in Gordon's view, was natural for the part. 'The problem's solved,' he proclaimed, but Kern resisted. Only when Max insisted Kern see Bob in action for himself was the casting assured.

In its pre-New York opening *Gowns by Roberta* stuck closely to the original story and even kept the same title. Hope took the part of Huckleberry Haines, the bandleader friend of John Kent, played by Ray Middleton, in the role made more famous a couple of years later by Fred Astaire, appearing with Ginger Rogers, in the film version of the show. The story concerns a young American couple who quarrel and go away to forget, both ending up in Paris. The boy's aunt runs a dress shop there, called Roberta, and he helps out. He inherits the shop on his aunt's death and takes over with the help of her young and attractive assistant. His former girlfriend arrives hoping they will get together again, but he has become attracted to the young assistant. They fall in love, and only later does he discover that she is a princess.

The show opened in Philadelphia in October 1933 to dismal reviews and lost $3,000 in its first week. It was said to be vague, slow-paced and lacking spontaneity. Gordon acted promptly, ordering re-writes and bringing in Hassard Short, a Broadway director with one of the finest reputations at that time, as well as firing Jerome Kern as director, though the songwriter was to remain to continue working on the show. The whole presentation was restaged and with great courage Gordon ordered new costumes and sets, putting the show $115,000 in the red before it even got to New York. Just before it opened at the New Amsterdam Theatre on Forty Second Street (the old Ziegfeld), the title was shortened to *Roberta*.

Unsettling as all these changes were, they gave Bob the chance to suggest improvements and develop his style.

Roberta opened in New York on 18 November, 1933, with a strong cast which included George Murphy, veteran Broadway star Fay Templeton, whom Max Gordon had tempted out of retirement, a beautiful Ukrainian called Tamara Drasin, Fred MacMurray, Alan Jones and Sidney Greenstreet.

The reviews were depressing. The losses piled high as attendances dropped. Then, just before Christmas, there came signs of a recovery. The upsurge continued as Kern's beautiful melody introduced in the show, 'Smoke gets in your Eyes', began to sweep the country. The best days were those just prior to Christmas, and throughout the New Year, spring and early summer the box office did roaring business. By midsummer audiences were falling again, and *Roberta* closed in New York on 21 July after 295 performances. By that time Bob had moved on to better-paid work, a parting no doubt induced by Gordon's anxiety to cut the cast's pay.

On Bob's own say-so, 'Much happened to me in the three years following *Roberta.*' He had his first real brush with the film industry, as a top star at the bottom end of the market, making two-reel comedy shorts in a studio at Astoria, Long Island, for Educational Films and later Warner Brothers. He also appeared in three Broadway shows within three years.

The filming began while he was still appearing in *Roberta,* providing a worthwhile boost to his income. He would film during the day and appear at the theatre in the evening. After *Roberta* closed, he appeared in *Say When* with Harry Richman at the Imperial (November 1934), *Ziegfeld Follies* with Josephine Baker, Fanny Brice and Gertrude Niesen at the Winter Garden (June 1936) and *Red, Hot and Blue* with Jimmy Durante and Ethel Merman at the Alvin (October 1936). Between his Broadway commitments he was kept busy with a succession of vaudeville dates. His radio work also increased. He featured on the Bromo Seltzer Show with Jane Froman and the Al Goodman Orchestra, and then with Shep Fields and his Rippling Rhythm Revue for Woodbury Soap. Picking up $2,500 for each two-reeler was a useful supplement to these other earnings, and for the first time in his career Bob was beginning to smile all the way to the bank.

It was during that spell in New York that he met Dolores

Reade for the first time. Dolores was building a reputation as a night-club singer and was then appearing with George Olsen's Band at the Vogue Club on 57th Street. Bob's close friend from the *Roberta* cast, George Murphy (who later left films to concentrate on politics, entering the US Senate in 1964), was responsible for their getting together, taking Bob to catch her act and introducing him to her.

Attracted by Dolores' good looks and captivated by her personality, Bob asked to see her home and on the way gave her tickets for *Roberta*. She was too embarrassed to go backstage after the performance, having assumed that he was only in the chorus. She hadn't realized he had such an important part. 'I sat in the audience scarcely breathing,' she explained later. After that they dated frequently, and when Dolores left with her mother for a singing date in Florida, the relationship continued by post. No sooner had she returned than Bob left for Cleveland to be with his mother, critically ill with cancer.

Then a gossip column news item which hinted that Bob was about to marry a chorus girl, and which appeared in print while he was out of town, threatened the romance. Bob insisted that the news was not true and explained that he hadn't even seen the girl since meeting Dolores. So the relationship progressed and on 19 February, 1934, Dolores Reade and Bob Hope were married at Erie, an unromantic industrial town not far from Cleveland and the shore of Lake Erie.

Bob was still appearing in *Roberta* when his mother died, her passing casting a cloud on what was otherwise probably the most successful and the happiest period of his professional and private life to that time. She had helped, inspired and encouraged him at times when she could so easily have been more conscious of her own needs, and was devoted to her large family of boys, always dutiful and loving. On all his travels, during the emotional highs and the depressing lows of struggling for recognition in vaudeville, he had kept in regular touch and even during the earlier days of meagre earnings had contrived to send money home. His mother had been a major influence in Bob's life, and he lost something of himself in her passing. One major regret and disappointment in his life is that she didn't live long enough to share his greatest successes. She did, however, appreciate the house in Cleveland which Bob bought for his parents, not far from their son Fred and his family.

Three years later Bob's father died, aged sixty-six. His decision to strike out for a new life in the United States more than twenty-five years before had changed the course of Bob's life, leading to his professional career on stage and worldwide fame in films. But he, too, missed Bob's most triumphant years.

3 The Great White Way

Bob Hope was late off the mark in moving to Hollywood. His *Road* co-stars were both there ahead of him. Crosby's first movie came out in 1930, and *The Big Broadcast*, his first film for Paramount, was released in 1932. Bob at his best, with all that matchless nonchalance, would likely as not explain that away by reminding us that Bing, after all, was much older than himself. In fact the difference was but two years. Lamour, too, beat him to Hollywood by two years, appearing in *The Jungle Princess* in 1936 — and Bob was eleven years her senior.

It's not that he didn't have the chance. The fact is that he was too comfortable, happy and busy and was finding life in New York too profitable to move. 'Hollywood? Who needs it?' he responded, turning a deaf ear to movie offers. 'The Broadway shows, radio, vaudeville and the movie shorts in New York were bringing in $5,000 a week, and the studios couldn't match that.' Nor was Dolores keen to move West. After their marriage she and Bob had built up an act together which was doing well.

But there was another, deeper reason. Bob was still bruised from Hollywood's dismissive attitude back in 1930 when, partnered by Louise Troxell, he had toured the West Coast unsuccessfully, playing, among a number of dates, the Hillstreet Theatre in Los Angeles. While there he was recommended to Bill Perlberg, a successful agent with strong contacts in the movie world, by Bob's first-ever gag-writer, Al Boasberg, whom he had used earlier while working at Proctors in New York.

Perlberg called Bob at his hotel. 'My friend Al Boasberg says you've got style. How would you like to make a test?' Knowing it wasn't sophisticated to be too eager, Bob played it cool. 'Let's see,' he responded. 'I have a little time between my closing at the Hillstreet and opening in San Diego. I think I could work it in.' The experienced Perlberg wasn't impressed or deceived, and simply told him to report to Pathé Studios the day after he closed at the Hillstreet if he was interested.

Bob and Louise took a cab out to Culver City, and he did his vaudeville act in front of the cameras. 'The crew seemed terribly amused, and I was certain that I was going to be Cleveland's gift to the motion picture world,' he said. But nothing happened. After he and Louise completed their engagement in San Diego and moved back to Los Angeles, Bob called Perlberg and asked him about the test. Bob said later: 'I could tell by the silence at the other end of the line that it hadn't exactly turned out like Ben Hur.' But Bob insisted and, despite Perlberg's attempt to dissuade him, was adamant about seeing the test. He joked later: 'Even the projectionist asked me if I really wanted to see it.'

There is no doubt that sitting totally on his own in a darkened room and for the first time in his life watching himself perform was a genuinely shattering experience which drained Bob's confidence. 'I was awful,' he said. 'I couldn't believe how bad I was. I knew my body had angles, but didn't realize how much they stuck out. When I made my first entrance, my nose came on screen ten minutes before the rest of my face.' At the end, when the lights came up, Bob felt so humiliated and shocked by the experience that he wished he could disappear on the spot. He said he slunk out of the projection room too embarrassed even to exit through the studio main gate. Instead he tried without success to scramble unnoticed over a side wall, which only added to his indignity. He said it was fully a week before he regained his confidence, but inwardly the experience hurt for a long time and left a scar on his sub-conscious which perhaps never totally healed.

Bob's 'ski-slope' nose, as it became popularly known, was mercilessly exploited over the coming years of verbal duelling with Crosby, and Bob proved himself in public balanced enough to use it for laughs in jokes against himself.

Seven years later, when the 'ski-slope' caused problems as Bob reported for work on his first feature movie, *The Big Broadcast of 1938,* it was tentatively suggested that he ought perhaps to consider surgery. Typically, he responded jokingly, saying that he and his nose had been together for a long time and hadn't done too badly so far. When make-up expert Wally Westmore pointed out that the camera would be coming up closer than any audience had seen him so far, Bob joked: 'You never played vaudeville.'

When Bob arrived home and told Dolores what had happened, she exploded, insisting that he must not let them talk him into any kind of surgery nonsense. 'I love your face the way it is. Your whole personality is in your face,' she insisted. When Bob casually mentioned to her that it might be in the best interests of his career to have something done about the nose, she still wouldn't hear of it, complaining that all they wanted to do was to turn him into just another stereotyped leading man. For a while the idea bubbled quietly under the surface at Paramount, but Dolores had her way and the profile remained intact.

That was long after Bob's unsuccessful screen-test at Paramount. Then his deep if irrational reaction to his own failure — since the blame could hardly be laid at Paramount's door — took the form of disdain for, if not outright contempt for and arrogance towards, Hollywood, a condition aggravated only shortly after his marriage to Dolores.

The couple were enjoying the fresh domesticity of being newly-weds and Dolores, in addition to making a home out of their three-bedroomed furnished apartment on Central Park West, was taking a close interest in Bob's professional life, encouraging him to search for a top-flight agent. He got one of the best, Louie 'Doc' Shurr, who put him up for the part of Huckleberry Haines in the already announced film version of *Roberta*. Bob's experience in the stage show must surely have put him in with a firm chance, but his rejection for a part he had already done — and which finally went to Fred Astaire — set him even more against the idea of a Hollywood career. Nor was an unhappy screen test at RKO for a featured spot in a Jack Oakie movie, to be shot in New York, designed to add any enchantment to the possibility of film-making.

After the closure of *Roberta* on stage, Bob could legitimately claim to be a Broadway star, but with no immediate follow-up planned, he developed an entirely new comedy routine with Dolores, and together they did a successful vaudeville tour of the eastern cities. Dolores loved it and later described it as an 'exciting and challenging experience'. For almost ten weeks they did as many as six or seven shows a day in a punishing schedule which, just occasionally, would leave Dolores' mind momentarily blank on stage. Bob, ever the perfectionist, would gag: 'What's the matter, you tired or something?'

Bob's astonishing capacity for work then, as later in life and into advanced years, was exceptional. He is a self-confessed 'owl', preferring to stay up until the early hours and not rising before ten, and is capable of sustaining an incredibly diverse schedule, dovetailing numerous business and charity responsibilities with arduous professional commitments.

In those New York days of early marriage, when Bob set about constructing a successful act with Dolores, he fastened onto a completely new presentation, engaging a couple of young and talented writers to work on some new ideas for his part of the programme, insisting that he should himself handle Dolores' script. The act gave Bob the opening with straight gagging. Then Dolores would sing her first song. By the time she started on her second number, Bob would be on stage once more and would proceed to distract her attention abominably by continuously clowning, most of it aimed at his overt attraction for her. Said Bob: 'I mooned over her, touched her arm, tasted her shoulder, did everything I could to break her up.' Dolores had a warm delivery, but Bob's fooling left the audience little opportunity to enjoy her songs, among them the evergreen 'Blue Moon'.

The act was fresh, and Bob's stand-up lines were topical, with perhaps the first hint of the benevolent satire which was to become the basis of his later performances. Audiences loved it, but it is doubtful if Bob and Dolores ever contemplated that act as being anything more than a convenient and happy interlude in his professional career. The stocky Louie Shurr, one of the most colourful, successful and aggressive agents of his day, saw Bob as a rising star and, while nothing had been decided, Bob was half expecting to be back on Broadway within a few months.

A show called *Say When,* about two entertainers who meet two sisters on an ocean liner and fall in love, brought Bob and Dolores back to New York after touring such important cities as Washington, Philadelphia and Boston. Harry Richman, one of the biggest names on Broadway in the 1930s, had agreed to put $50,000 into the show on condition that Hope be his co-star and wasn't over-concerned when he discovered that Bob had most of the best lines. Or so it seemed.

After pre-runs in Boston, *Say When* opened at the Imperial in New York in November 1934. Reviews were good, and there seemed no reason why it should not enjoy a long run, but off-stage bickering got in the way. Librettist Jack McGowan and composer Ray Henderson were convinced that, with more co-operation from Richman, they had a winner. Richman, on the other hand, and against their wishes, wanted to improve his own part substantially. The dispute led to the show's sad decline and arguably to its premature closure once Richman, who had the controlling financial interest, made up his mind to pull out.

Bob got on well with Richman and, having been kept in touch with the situation, was not surprised when *Say When* folded. It would be some eighteen months before he was working on Broadway again, but a major radio series, film shorts shot in New York, and a successful series of stage dates with Dolores provided a busy and demanding schedule, so he was not unduly put out by the show's demise.

Bob was still doggedly anti-Hollywood, but a series of events was beginning to take shape which would lead him to the West Coast, to his first major film and the chance to make good in a new career. Once that sequence of events started, it advanced with dazzling speed.

Bob's agent, Louie Shurr, was the instigator, when he negotiated the leading male comedy role for Bob in a new edition of *Ziegfeld Follies*. With him was a star-studded cast which included Fanny Brice, Ken Murray, Josephine Baker, Gertrude Niesen, Edgar Bergen and Charlie McCarthy, Judy Canova and the Nicholas Brothers. It also featured a girl who was to cast a great influence on Bob's future, a then little-known vivacious twenty-two-year-old showgirl called Eve Arden.

Ten years later Eve was to win an Oscar nomination for her portrayal of Joan Crawford's wise-cracking friend in the film classic *Mildred Pierce,* and later still an Emmy award as television's top comedienne, but back in 1935 she shared a vitally important scene with Hope. Vernan Duke and Ira Gershwin had penned a beautiful melody for the show called 'I Can't Get Started with You'. It later became a jazz-inspired standard through the interpretive skills and sensitive virtuosity of trumpeter Bunny Berigan, but in *Ziegfeld Follies* Bob sang the number to Eve Arden, and it became the show's biggest hit.

Prior to the 1930s Florenz Ziegfeld had been the impresario of the day, with an enormous reputation for mounting spectacular shows known for their extravagance and expense and a proliferation of long-legged, scantily attired showgirls parading in a series of harmlessly aphrodisiac settings. Ruined by the

Wall Street Crash, he died in 1932, after having master-minded some twenty-four editions of *Ziegfeld Follies. Ziegfeld Follies of 1935,* intended to acknowledge the genius of Flo Ziegfeld, after projecting much pre-opening promise, sadly faltered almost from the start, its level of success never able to justify the great man's memory. Co-produced by the Shubert brothers, Lee and John, and Ziegfeld's widow, Billie Burke, this latest and sup-posedly greatest *Follies* of them all ran into early casting problems, forcing a two-month delay. Its eventual opening at Christmas at the Boston Opera House showed it to be over-long. Ken Murray was forced out, but not before an acrimonious dispute with Louie Shurr over whether he or Bob Hope was top billing. Later when more cuts were necessary Edgar Bergen and Charlie McCarthy were sacrificed. Such tensions notwith-standing, the show coasted along nicely until Fanny Brice's illness forced a temporary closure.

Bob turned down the offer to re-join the *Follies* cast when the show resumed in the late summer, but the number he did with Eve Arden had already been seen by Mitchell Leisen and Harlan Thompson, who were later to direct and produce *The Big Broadcast of 1938.* They saw Hope's potential for the first time in the *Follies* and later wanted him for Hollywood. But in 1936 Bob was still outwardly unimpressed by any possibility of a film career. He saw too many opportunities for himself right there in good old New York. It was by far his favourite place.

Even before the opening of the *Follies* Bob had started to build a reputation as a radio comedian, appearing first on the RKO *Theatre of the Air* programme and then with the beautiful Honey Chile Wilder on the *Bromo Seltzer Intimate Hour.* He had also been in the happy position of being able to pick up whatever bookings he wanted for himself and Dolores through the Loew circuit. So the *Follies'* temporary closure was by no means a disaster. In fact, Louie Shurr was already negotiating for him to appear in a new Broadway musical comedy. In the meantime Bob was able to take the chance to do more radio work and mixed this in with a crippling schedule of one-night benefits. He also decided to exercise his option to appear in a couple more film shorts re-leased in 1936 for Warner Brothers.

The opportunity to do comedy shorts had first arisen in 1934 after Bob turned down the chance to appear with Jack Oakie in a feature film being made by RKO. Said Bob: 'The offer for the movie shorts came from Educational, which made two-reelers at a studio in Astoria, Long Island. The producer, Jack Skirball, was willing to give me $2,500 per short and I was supposed to make six of them. I could work in *Roberta* at night and make the shorts in the daytime.'

The films were never meant for posterity. The first, called *Going Spanish*, had Bob swallowing some Mexican jumping beans and, with his co-star, Leah Ray, cavorting around the set. Bob had never expected it to be a classic but after seeing it on opening day at the Rialto Theatre in New York, he was appalled. It was the projection room at Pathé in 1930 all over again.

Bob's gut reaction to it, when he left the theatre and immediately bumped into famous New York columnist Walter Winchell, cost him his contract with Educational. He and Winchell had known one another for years, and when Walter asked him how his film début had gone, Bob responded instinctively and, predictably, with a telling one-liner: 'I'll tell you how it was. When they catch John Dillinger, they're going to make him sit through it twice' — Dillinger being New York's Public Enemy Number 1 at the time. Bob might have been naïve, but it was the sort of quote on which the shrewd Winchell had built his reputation, and when Bob's comment appeared in print verbatim to be read by thousands, including not least significantly Educational's Jack Skirball himself, his time with Educational was virtually at an end.

Skirball phoned Louie Shurr: 'What the hell is your client doing to us? Bob Hope is hard enough to sell without him running down his own picture in Winchell's column. We're through with him! We're dropping his option.' At Shurr's request Bob tried to get Winchell to print a retraction, but how could he? As he pointed out to Bob: 'I only printed what you said.'

Fortunately, not long after, Warner Brothers stepped in with an offer. They were scheduled to do a shortened version of Cole Porter's 1929 success *Fifty Million Frenchmen*, to be shot conveniently for Bob at Warner's Eastern Studio in Brooklyn. The re-shoot emerged as *Paree, Paree*, and Bob's co-stars included Dorothy Stone, who had appeared in New York in a number of shows, including *Stepping Stones*, with her father, Fred Stone, and with Fred Astaire as Claire Luce's replacement in the

1932 Broadway hit *Gay Divorce.*

It was perhaps in *Paree, Paree* that Bob's remarkable knack of becoming associated with hit songs began. In the film he had the good fortune of singing 'You Do Something To Me' to Dorothy Stone. It turned out to be one of Cole Porter's best-ever ballads and was set to become an all-time pop standard.

Going Spanish had taught Bob an important lesson when dealing with the Press, so after *Paree, Paree,* whatever his opinion of the film or his own performance might have been, there was no choice titbit for Winchell's column to spoil what Warners obviously felt was an encouraging performance. They quickly took up his option and put him in five more twenty-minute comedy shorts over the next two years. In 1935 he did *The Old Grey Mayor, Watch the Birdie* (cast as a wise-cracking lover) and *Double Exposure,* a farce based on photography. In 1936 he added *Calling All Tars,* not surprisingly about the ability of men in sailor suits to pull the girls, and *Shop Talk,* with a department-store background.

These superficial pot-boilers, all directed by Lloyd French, gave Bob useful experience of working in front of the camera but could hardly be claimed to have set him firmly on the road to Hollywood. But even if instinctively Bob was still resisting the lure of films, he was forced to acknowledge the gathering impact of the medium as more and more Broadway stars were drawn away on the promise of new and exciting opportunities in Hollywood.

The defection was taking place under his very nose. He felt it most strongly when his co-stars from *Roberta,* Fred MacMurray and George Murphy, left — Fred after a successful screen test in New York for Paramount, for which he borrowed Bob's black silk topper to go with his hired evening dress, and George to take up a Columbia Pictures contract.

Despite his deep-seated resentment of Hollywood, Bob began for the first time to think more seriously about films. He didn't relish the idea of being left out of what was becoming a fashionable trend. It struck home strongly when Louie Shurr, within earshot of Bob in his Times Square office, told George Murphy about his movie contract and to pack his bags for Hollywood. Bob admitted to feeling envious: 'I turned to Murph and said that, if it could happen to him, then maybe it could happen to me.' Against some of his natural instincts he asked Louie Shurr to see what he could do.

Earlier Bob had followed too hectic a schedule to worry over-much about Hollywood. In 1936, after *Ziegfeld Follies of 1935,* Shurr had secured him high billing in the part of Bob Hale in *Red, Hot and Blue!* The storyline was not strong, but hopes for the new show ran high. It was intended as a follow-up to the highly successful *Anything Goes* of two years before, which had done phenomenal business with an impressive 420 performances before closing. Producer Vincent Freedley and director Howard Lindsay reckoned that, if they brought together as much as possible of the talent which had made *Anything Goes* such a hit, they would stand a good chance of having another successful show on their hands. Ethel Merman was recruited, along with Russell Crouse and William Gaxton. Cole Porter was brought in to write a new score.

Bob's chance came when Gaxton left the show long before opening night. He had allegedly walked in on a meeting which was discussing Merman's part and from which he deduced, probably quite rightly, that his own part was being subordinated. He stormed out and straight into another, even bigger Broadway role. It was a significant omen, for after Jimmy Durante had been brought in, he and Ethel Merman argued against each other in their claim for top billing. Their astonishingly eccentric dual billing, which had their names criss-crossing diagonally above the title, solved the problem. Even then, to maintain absolute parity, the names had to be transposed every two weeks. Bob's billing was never in doubt or challenged. His name also appeared above the title.

Before the New York opening there were other problems. The story was constantly being revised, it was far too long, songs were being cut and at one stage Cole Porter walked out, though he was persuaded to return after a New Haven try-out when critics blamed his score for some of the failings. At one point Bob's position became vulnerable and he had to send in Louie Shurr to do battle with Lindsay and Crouse to avoid being taken out of the first-act finale. Nonetheless, *Red, Hot and Blue!* opened at the Alvin Theatre on 29 October, 1936 triumphantly, with generous advance bookings, and continued to do brisk business well into 1937.

Red, Hot and Blue! gave Bob the chance to indulge his talent for the topical ad-lib, an inclination which brought increasing anxiety for Lindsay and Crouse and occasional momentary panic for Merman. But it was with Merman that Bob developed his knack of singing songs which were to remain in public memory. Porter's score, by general consensus not as sparkling as might have been expected — he had written his first Broadway hit, *Paris,* as early as 1928 — did nevertheless include one memorable tune which Bob and Merman sang as a duet. The delightful 'It's De-Lovely' was said to have been written just a short time before, for the 1936-released MGM musical *Born to Dance,* starring Eleanor Powell, James Stewart and Frances Langford, but not used. When brought out again for *Red, Hot and Blue!,* it might not have had such an immediate impact as some of the show's other songs, but it lasted much longer and remained a Cole Porter standard long after the others faded from public memory.

Despite its problems, Hope enjoyed *Red, Hot and Blue!* He admired the obvious talents of Ethel Merman and Jimmy Durante and, with the latter particularly, built up an entertaining relationship. Together they appeared at a number of benefit shows, this period initiating a friendship which was to endure for more than forty years. Though their styles were different, their careers did perhaps have a common core. Durante had first appeared on Broadway in 1929 and made a host of movies, most of them largely undistinguished except for his own special brand of brash and effervescent humour, but the impression remained that he was always more suited to the warmth and intimacy of a live audience. He was difficult to pigeon-hole, but forced into an assessment it would be hard not to put him down as essentially one of the great vaudeville entertainers.

Bob Hope certainly created much more impact on film, rising tall above Durante in the *Road* series, but in the perspective of his sixty-odd years in show business, he too is hard to classify. Some would argue that, for all his success on radio, through personal appearances, in the cinema and on television, he also remains essentially an outstanding vaudevillian.

However, that's not to say that Bob's style and approach had not developed since his early days on stage. He was now, at the time of *Red, Hot and Blue!,* thirty-three years old and had been 'in the business' for some fourteen years. When he first partnered George Byrne, in 1926, they became known for their eccentric dance routines, but in an attempt to broaden their appeal they began to inject a few comedy lines. By later standards their jokes were basic and unsophisticated, but they were intended solely to raise a laugh and more often than not, in those days, did.

George would walk across the stage with a wooden plank under his arm. Bob, as the straight man, would ask him where he was going. George: 'To find a room. I've already got my board.' Hope would ask Byrne where bugs went in the winter. 'Search me,' responded Byrne.

Simple jokes brought the laughs, but it wasn't long before Bob began developing his own special style of comedy, often mockingly taking audiences into his confidence by putting himself on their side in ridiculing, or putting one over on, his partner. Time smoothed out the rough edges, the delivery became more precise and convincing, the timing impeccable, and the whole routine more professional and sophisticated. By 1936 he was using the services of three gag-writers, mainly for his radio work, and it was estimated that he had a collection of 80,000 jokes. There were still plenty of obvious, instant one-liners, but his material was now smoother and often more subtle. With more experience came the audacity to swap banter with stage partners, often for the benefit of his audience but at times for his own amusement.

The classic case, told in *Bob Hope, A Life of Comedy* by William Robert Faith, concerns Jimmy Durante during an impromptu performance at the Lake Shore Athletic Club. Bob was in the middle of his parade of jokes when he spotted Durante just off stage signing a few autographs before making for home, his performance over for the night. Bob seized his opportunity and announced that the audience must surely have heard enough of him, Bob Hope, so 'Let's bring back Jimmy Durante,' he called. The audience responded, cheering and shouting for Jimmy's return. Durante came on stage to take what he hoped would be just a few final bows, but Bob had the bit between his teeth. 'We can't let him get away without your favourite number,' he called, and the audience took up the call. There was no alternative: Jimmy was left to do his encore. Thereupon Bob walked off stage and out of the theatre and took a cab back to his hotel. But Jimmy took it in good part.

After, *Red, Hot and Blue!* ended its run after just a couple of weeks at the Civic Opera House in Chicago in May 1937, Bob successfully auditioned for the master of ceremonies spot in the important *Rippling Rhythm Revue* on NBC radio, with a refreshing new format put together in less than a week, and based on the monologue approach. The style made him different from all other comedians, and he gained good reviews including *Variety*'s apt: 'Hope added enough fresh chatter and gags to give the entire broadcast a lift . . .'

Bob's impact on radio was obvious, his contract was extended substantially, and he began to think that radio was perhaps his natural medium, though filming didn't altogether take a back seat. In 1937 he made what turned out to be an historic short, playing himself at a golf tournament. Appearing with Bob was Bing Crosby. It was the first time they worked together in a motion picture,

That same year, over in Hollywood, director Mitchell Leisen and producer Harlan Thompson were working on a new film called *The Big Broadcast of 1938*. It was much the fashion then to stick with a winning theme once you had found one and the first *Big Broadcast* movie to be screened as one of the series came out in 1936, though its origins were set in the 1930 movie *Paramount on Parade,* a film revue format given the spectacular Hollywood treatment and featuring a host of stars in a succession of comedy sketches, big production numbers and songs. The idea was to get as many top names into the programme as possible. The re-make in 1936 followed the vaudeville theme and featured a string of the biggest names of the day including Jack Oakie, George Burns and Gracie Allen, Bing Crosby, Ethel Merman, Bill Robinson, the Nicholas Brothers, Amos 'n' Andy, Charles Ruggles, Richard Tauber and Ray Noble and his Band. It was so extravagantly produced that it was a financial flop. This didn't prevent Paramount making a follow-up, *The Big Broadcast of 1937,* which featured Jack Benny, Martha Raye, George Burns and Gracie Allen, Shirley Ross and Ray Milland with Benny Goodman's clarinet and Larry Adler's harmonica playing.

This time the film made money, and plans were quickly laid to cash in with *The Big Broadcast of 1938.* But Mitchell Leisen and Harlan Thompson were soon in a dilemma: their first and second choice for top starring roles both turned them down. They were anxiously looking around for someone else they could approach when they remembered the Shubert Brothers' production of *Ziegfeld Follies of 1936,* a couple of years before on

Broadway. They remembered the hit of the show, 'I Can't Get Started With You', sung to Eve Arden and with some significance for the future progress of our story, they remembered the man who had sung the song . . . Bob Hope.

4 The Road West

Hope went to Hollywood willingly enough, but he wasn't sure if it would work out in the long term. He knew that his New York based reputation as a stage and radio performer, though impressive, would count for nothing in the movies and that he would need to learn new techniques and build his own screen persona if he was ever going to make an impact in Hollywood.

Paramount had offered him a good deal: a seven-year contract, with options, for three pictures a year at $20,000 for each picture — he could not have wished for more. But he remained defensive, unsure and tentative about Hollywood, inhibited by the legacy of his earlier unfortunate contacts. He firmly told his agent, Louie 'Doc' Shurr, that the options could work both ways and that if he didn't feel happy he could call it a day after the first picture and take Dolores hot-foot back to New York. He didn't see pictures as essential to his professional future. Undoubtedly, the inner drive to succeed was there and Bob responded positively to the challenge of an exciting new medium, but his now solid reputation in sound broadcasting gave him an element of independence. His twenty-six week contract as host of the *Woodbury Soap Show,* signed in May 1937, still had a couple of months to run and he was a big enough name for the company to arrange for him to continue doing the show from California, via a special transcontinental link.

It was September 1937 when Bob and Dolores arrived in Hollywood and within a few days he was on the set of *The Big Broadcast of 1938.* W.C. Fields, the Philadelphia-born star with a rare genius for combining pathos with his own brand of comic interpretation, was the big draw, appearing in his first picture since recovering from illness. Hope was down the cast list in sixth place, behind Fields, Martha Raye, Dorothy Lamour, Shirley Ross and Lynne Overman.

The picture was the fourth, and turned out to be the last, in the *Big Broadcast* musical series and was never credited for its storyline. Bob himself got it about right with his now legendary quip: *'Variety* is offering a $10,000 prize for anyone who can describe the plot.' But this musical adaptation of a story by Frederick Hazlitt Brennan was a very adequate if unambitious film review of a kind then popular, with various turns and guest artists. As such it rated well, inspiring one reviewer at the time to claim it as a 'gorgeously entertaining mixture of mirth, melody, spectacle, song, fun, frolic, dance and dazzle, magnificently mounted and streamlined for speed'. This review was certainly not alone in ignoring Hope's presence in the cast. Another, after claiming that 'Martha Raye is as raucous as ever' and that 'Dorothy Lamour and Shirley Ross look charming', suggested that the supporting players were given few opportunities.

Some reviews, however, did acknowledge Hope's potential. One announced that: 'Shirley Ross sings and dances and adds romance and Bob Hope, who at times looks remarkably like Jack Benny, makes his first appearance in a very promising featured part.' And another: 'Shirley Ross and Bob Hope put over "Thanks for the Memory", the best number in films I have heard for many months', later commending the film for 'the agreeable work of these two artists'.

If Jack Benny's turning down the part of Buzz Fielding in *The Big Broadcast of 1938* was one remarkable stroke of fortune for Bob Hope, then Dorothy Lamour's fondness for him and her faith in his ability to become a star must certainly have been another. Although the song 'Thanks for the Memory' had been written for Bob Hope and Shirley Ross, Dotty could easily have secured it for herself. When going through the whole score of the picture with director Mitchell Leisen before shooting had begun, she instantly identified the Ralph Rainger, Leo Robin number as a potential hit. She claimed that Leisen said he would switch things if she really wanted to do the number, but as that would have involved some re-writing, she said she would rather Bob do it. 'I wanted Bob to sing it and I'm glad I turned the song down,' she said later. 'I would never have done as much for that tune as Bob did.'

Bob remembers Mitch Leisen for other reasons too. In the early days of *Big Broadcast* he took Bob to lunch at Lacey's, the Paramount studio's watering hole, to give him some useful tips on movie acting. He explained how important the eyes are in film-making. 'All the great movie actors say their lines with their eyes before they say them with their mouths. Remember, think the emotion and it will register in your eyes.' Bob took the lesson to heart when he shared the hit song with Shirley Ross. 'When I saw the rushes, I was astonished at my galloping orbs,' he explained years later. 'Even today when I see the "Thanks for the Memory" number, I cringe.' But it was good advice.

It was Leisen, too, who astutely decided to slow down the pace of 'Thanks for the Memory'. Rainger and Robin had written it as a much quicker number, but Leisen saw its greater potential if taken at a slower tempo. Having set the mood by the tempo, he then brought the full Paramount orchestra onto the set and ordered a direct recording. The story goes that at the end of the scene Ralph Rainger and Leo Robin were so delighted that they were in tears, and the crew broke into spontaneous applause. Hope liked the number from the start, his matching with Shirley Ross seemed faultless, and 'Thanks for the Memory' was destined to win the Academy Award for the best film song of 1938.

Shirley Ross, the oval-faced redhead with appealing eyes, occupies a favoured place in any Bob Hope story for she shared what was to be the turning point in his career. Underrated as a film celebrity, the girl from Omaha, Nebraska, was hardly noticed until she appeared with Hope in *The Big Broadcast of 1938,* though she had given an attractive performance as a small town girl boosted to stardom on the stage in 1936 in the 1937 *Big Broadcast.*

Though Shirley was to go on to make another nine films after her teaming with Hope in the movie song 'Thanks for the Memory', she sadly never fully escaped from her earlier reputation as a fine musician and band singer. Her family had moved to New York and then to Los Angeles when she was a child and she was educated in Hollywood. Music and acting were her main interests. Her style of piano playing and blues-influenced singing attracted the attention of bandleader Gus Arnheim, and it was while she was appearing with Arnheim's orchestra in their regular spot at the fashionable Beverly Wilshire Hotel in Hollywood that she was signed by MGM in 1933, when she was probably just out of her teens.

For three years Shirley Ross was cast in minor roles. She made her film début in 1933 in *Bombshell,* which starred Jean Harlow, though she was so far down the cast list that nobody noticed her. She made five films in 1934, three more in 1935, all for MGM, but after *San Francisco* early in 1936 she switched to Paramount, who cleverly softened her screen image by giving her a better, kinder make-up and gentler honey-blonde hair. After two more films that year, including *The Big Broadcast of 1937*, she made *Hideaway Girl* with Martha Raye and Robert Cummings, *Waikiki Wedding*, the big Bing Crosby hit, and *Blossoms on Broadway* with Edward Arnold, before *The Big Broadcast of 1938* brought her together with Hope for the first time and the famous duet to the screen.

It is disappointing and unjust that Shirley Ross, who contributed so much to the film which pointed Hope firmly towards film stardom, should have been treated so shabbily by movie historians. She appears to have enjoyed only marginal, fleeting recognition, and most accounts of Hope's career give scant attention to his important co-star, whose obvious talents as a singer, musician, actress and tongue-in-cheek comedienne deserved a stronger place in the memory of Hollywood. She was popular on radio in America in the Bob Burns shows and in *Anything Goes* on the West Coast and, of course, shared with Bob the phenomenal success of 'Thanks for the Memory' when the song was released on record. That year, 1938, she married her agent, Ken Dolan, who died in 1951. They had two sons, and she had a daughter from her second marriage, to Edward Blum. Shirley Ross died of cancer in a Californian convalescent hospital in March 1975.

Shirley looked a little like Jean Arthur, and perhaps that was a disadvantage, but Hope recognized her talent as she did his. She was convinced that nobody could weigh up the potential of a joke as accurately as he could. They made two more films together, the hurriedly put-together *Thanks for the Memory*, pushed through to exploit their earlier success, and *Some Like It Hot*, released in May 1939. She enjoyed the fun of making a movie with Hope. 'I know of no one who can match Bob's capacity for work and play at the same time,' she said later.

The success of the Bob Hope-Shirley Ross song wasn't apparent immediately shooting had been completed. Box-office reaction to the picture was by no means sure. Certainly, Paramount didn't see the film or the song as an immediate breakthrough for Hope, and although they considered his work competent and the song pleasant enough, he wasn't at that point, in 1937, identified as star material. But they took up their option and cast him in a fluffy comedy musical called *College Swing* with George Burns and Gracie Allen, Martha Raye, Edward Everett Horton, Ben Blue, Betty Grable, Jackie Coogan, John Payne and Jerry Colonna. His part was so small to start with that he considered packing his bags and returning with Dolores to New York. So upset was he that in desperation he got producer Lewis Gensler to beef up the part. (Gensler had produced Hope's first Broadway show, *Ballyhoo of 1932*.) His role as the brash Bud Brady gave him an attractive duet with Martha Raye called 'How 'dya Like to Love Me?' It wasn't as big as 'Thanks for the Memory', nor was it the top tune from the film, but it was pleasant enough and became quite a hit for a time.

College Swing, called *Swing, Teacher Swing* in Britain, was about a girl who inherits a small-town college and brings in vaudeville stars to give the lessons — hardly an inspiring plot, and not likely to put Hope's career on the next rung of the ladder of success. But it did just manage to keep him at Paramount, who now cast him in another low-budget picture called *Give Me a Sailor*. This didn't advance his career either. Co-starring again with Martha Raye and Betty Grable was a lot of fun, conceded Bob, but the film had a diabolical plot about a couple of sisters' romances with two sailors. Apart from a pleasant song called 'What Goes on Here in my Heart?' which maintained his reputation for being in films with songs which scored heavily with the public, the film is best forgotten.

Bob Hope's career as a film star might easily have ended at this point. His contract with Paramount was so much in the balance that while he waited to hear from them he sent his agents out shopping for other deals, because by now he was determined to stick it out in Hollywood, his morale boosted by a radio career which was putting him well up with such top comedians of the day as Jack Benny, Fred Allen and Edgar Bergen. Universal came up with an offer which would give him $10,000 a picture, just half the value of his contract with Paramount — if he had a contract with Paramount! According to Hope, Walter Wanger agreed to hire him for a comedy called *Bedtime Story*. 'The only hurdle was Loretta Young, who had approval of her co-star. She chose David Niven,' he said.

Paramount were taking a long time to come to terms with Hope's potential. But while he had been making *College Swing*, released in April 1938, and *Give Me a Sailor*, released just four months later, his reputation among the paying public had been mounting. The turn came in early March 1938 when most of America's top columnists reviewed *The Big Broadcast of 1938*. Ed Sullivan, Hedda Hopper, Louella Parsons and Walter Winchell were all enthusiastic about 'Thanks for the Memory' and marked Hope's card as a candidate for film stardom. A week later Damon Runyon raved about the song in his widely syndicated column and wrote glowingly of Hope's performance. It was Bob's first outright critical success since moving into films and contributed to his choice of the song as his signature tune some time later.

Bob's press agent put a copy of Runyon's glowing full-column review on the desk of William LeBaron, head of production at Paramount, but until the influence of this shrewd move paid off, Paramount dithered, more inclined to judge from the financial take registered by a picture rather than Press reviews or record sales. Bob was so uncertain about the future that he took up the chance to make a triumphant return to the stage, re-creating his role of Huckleberry Haines in a West Coast première of *Roberta* in Los Angeles. In the cast this time was a young starlet named Carole Landis, who later emerged as one of the most glamorous Hollywood stars of the 1940s.

By design or coincidence, when their decision was made, Paramount conveyed it with impeccable timing. On the day *Roberta* opened at the Philharmonic Auditorium — a glittering occasion attended by Jerome Kern, who had produced new songs for the revival — the studio telephoned Louie Shurr to say that Paramount had decided to take up Hope's contract and were making immediate plans to pair him once again with Shirley Ross in *Thanks for the Memory*. It was ironic that, after all the doubts and frustrations Bob had experienced while waiting for Paramount to make up their mind, it was now their turn to wait because he in the meantime had signed to do a summer vaudeville tour working with Dolores, who looked after the songs, and with Jackie Coogan (who incidentally was married to Betty Grable) helping him with the comedy. They opened on Broadway in June and didn't get back to California until mid-July.

It was hardly a triumphant return professionally, though at this point Bob and Dolores were sufficiently settled about the future that they decided to make their home in Los Angeles, moving all their furniture and belongings over from New York.

Bob had hoped that *Thanks for the Memory* would be new and

exciting, with Paramount willing to back it strongly in a positive effort to capitalize on the success of the title song from the earlier picture. He was disappointed to find that it wasn't a prime movie in Paramount's estimation, the budget allocation was low, and the film was a re-hash of a 1931 movie called *Up Pops the Devil,* which featured Carole Lombard. The screenplay by Lynn Starling, from a stage play by Albert Hackett and Frances Goodrich, was about a couple of newlyweds, she a former model, he an aspiring author. So that he can concentrate on writing they decide she should return to modelling, but it doesn't work out, they quarrel and then separate. The traumatic experience nonetheless inspires him to complete his book. It was a good-natured comedy, well received, and the pairing of Bob Hope and Shirley Ross once again inspired a hit song — with a little help from Hoagy Carmichael, who wrote the music, and Frank Loesser, who penned the words. The all-time standard, 'Two Sleepy People', sung by Bob and Shirley in the film, was a huge success, the record of the song by the co-stars going on to sell more than a million copies.

Musically, if in no other way, Hope was now knocking hard on Paramount's door. Two major hit songs in the space of ten months were certain to get him noticed. But, in fairness to Paramount, they couldn't have known at this point what the full impact of 'Two Sleepy People' would be. All they did was offer Bob roles in two more B movies.

Never Say Die, released in April 1939, co-starred Bob Hope once more with Martha Raye. He played the part of a cranky millionaire given a month to live. To avoid the clutches of an adventuress, he marries Martha Raye, who is retreating from the unwanted attentions of a distasteful prince. Bob marries her so that she will inherit his fortune (and can then marry the man she really wants), but of course he survives, and she decides she wants to share her life with him. It wasn't the kind of film to earn much praise from the critics, but the public found it entertaining, and it did reasonably well at the box office.

Sensing now that 'Two Sleepy People' could well become a hit, Paramount put Shirley and Bob together once more in a hurried re-write of a Ben Hecht-Gene Fowler play called *The Green Magoo.* The fact that the play had folded after only eleven performances on Broadway hadn't prevented the picture industry's taking it up in 1934, when Paramount put it out as

Shoot the Works (*Thank Your Stars* in the UK), with Jack Oakie.
The latest effort, released in May 1939, was adapted by Lewis R. Foster and, in addition to Hope and Ross, starred Una Merkel, Gene Krupa and Richard Denning. The studio put it out under the name *Some Like It Hot,* (not to be confused with the 1959 box-office hit of the same name which featured Marilyn Monroe, Jack Lemmon and Tony Curtis). In the end it was a languid attempt at consolidating what would seem to have been the substantial potential of the Hope-Ross pairing. 'The Lady's in Love with You', a melodic song, was probably the brightest thing in a picture about a sideshow owner and his many ideas to raise money, which never reached what seemed at one point to have excellent potential. It was also the last picture Bob and Shirley did together.

Bob Hope said later: '*Some Like It Hot* was the rock bottom point in my movie career. After that one there was no place to go but up.'

Such material wasn't likely to capture the attention of the studio bosses at Paramount, or of any other studio for that matter, but they were forced to take note of Bob's advancing career on radio. After the *Woodbury Soap Show,* where he was billed as 'America's Cleanest Comedian', he had appeared with Dick Powell in the *Lucky Strike Show,* but the big opportunity came in 1938 when a major advertising agency, Lord & Thomas, were looking for someone to take over from Amos 'n' Andy. Bob was successful. It was an important breakthrough and he was determined to make an impact, for the show benefited from the major sponsorship of Pepsodent Toothpaste. He marshalled a small army of young and talented scriptwriters and worked hard himself pulling the show into shape and creating something different, a kind of comedy that was crazier and in its own way much cleverer than anything heard before.

Bob's accelerating radio career, along with his growing popularity as the most polished and professional master of ceremonies in Hollywood — early in 1938 he was asked for the first time to be a presenter at the Academy Award ceremonies — gave him the higher profile he needed to make the Paramount bosses take notice. 'They began to take another look at the guy who was making those B pictures with Martha Raye and Shirley Ross,' he declared.

By general consensus, *The Cat and the Canary* was the break he had been looking for — 'the turning point in my movie career', said Hope. It was his seventh film for Paramount and the first to be planned and produced to showcase his comedy talent. Chosen to co-star with him was Paulette Goddard, who, after appearing in Hal Roach shorts in 1929, had starred with Charles Chaplin in *Modern Times* in 1936 and as a predatory female in *The Women,* which led to a contract with Paramount. *The Cat and the Canary* made her a big star and proved to be the turning point of her career also. Her performance won her a film contract which made her one of Hollywood's biggest stars for some ten years.

There had been two previous screen versions of John Willard's old haunted house classic — a silent version in 1927 and Universal's *The Cat Creeps* in 1930. With Hope in mind, screenwriters Walter De Leon and Lynn Starling's rewrite was competent and bright, giving the old Broadway melodrama additional comedy which Bob handled superbly. Deft touches from Elliott Nugent gave the film good pace and direction, and although the running time was but 72 minutes, it provided Bob with exactly the right opportunity to establish himself almost overnight as a film comedian of stature.

The heroine, played by Paulette Goddard, has been left a fortune by an eccentric millionaire and is subsequently terrified by a number of no-gooders who want to get their hands on the money. The melodramatic style is retained and includes a spooky mansion, weird happenings and three murders, but the hero, played by Bob Hope, despite his own obvious fear manages to solve the murders. The film was not only excellent entertainment, hugely successful for Hope and Goddard and a commercial success, but it put down a definite marker to the *Road* films yet to come.

For the first time, a Hope film took up the essential elements of the individual type of comedy which had given him star billing on radio. It captured the essence of his quick-witted, stand-up style of delivery, the essential Hope spontaneity, and enabled him to project himself in the unconventional lady-killer image which was developed cleverly in the *Road* films, with Crosby invariably ending up with the girl. As film-writer Janice Anderson so succinctly put it in her book, *History of Movie Comedy, The Cat and the Canary* provided the perfect part to let Hope display 'his comedy persona of faint-hearted cowardice, tottering bravado and shining egotism; and plenty of room for the wisecracks and gags that have always been his hallmark.'

Hope classics peppered a tightly written script, as when a lady asks him if big empty houses scare him: 'Not me . . . I was in vaudeville,' and, 'I always joke when I'm scared; I kid myself that I'm brave.' Perhaps the most typical of Hope and a personal favourite was, 'My mother brought me up never to be caught twice in the same lady's bedroom.'

It was the sort of stuff which Bob had been developing success-fully on radio, transmitted without loss of impact or effect, to film, a combination that brought out the best of his vaudeville and radio techniques. The characteristics were crystal clear — the quick joke when confronted by a difficult situation; the 'great lover' guise while lacking the looks, physique, technique and staying power of the real thing; the reluctant yet gratified hero and go-getter — excelling in the joys and perks of the role but back-tracking and squirming when required to measure up to the image.

The formula won critical acclaim. The best and possibly the most apt review appeared in the *Motion Picture Herald:* 'Para-mount here has solved for itself, exhibitors and customers, the heretofore perplexing problem of what to do with Bob Hope, admittedly one of the funniest comedians who ever faced a camera, yet never until now the sure-fire laugh-getter on the screen that his following knew him to be in fact!' Bob was thrilled and delighted that at last his movie career seemed to be on course.

Hope enjoyed making the film. He thought Paulette Goddard 'beautiful and talented'. One of the precious moments of his life about this time was when he came across Paulette and her then husband, Charles Chaplin, at the Santa Anita race track. Chaplin had been a prime inspiration during Bob's vaudeville days and he had once waited in a New York street for an hour and a half just to catch a glimpse of the great comedian. Paulette made the introduction casually enough: 'You know Charles, don't you?' Said Bob: 'I gulped. There in front of me was the legend. Twenty years before, I had imitated him and won prizes for it at home in Cleveland.' Chaplin told Hope that he had been watching the rushes of *The Cat and the Canary* and that he was one of the best timers of comedy he had ever seen.

The European War which had been threatening during the making of *The Cat and the Canary* had become reality before the major reviews hit the streets, and Bob and Dolores narrowly escaped being part of the early conflict. Shooting on the film had ended in May 1939 and his last Pepsodent radio show in the current series was due on 20 June. There was time for a vacation, to satisfy Dolores' long-held ambition to visit Paris and for them to visit his relatives in Britain. It would be Bob's first return to the old country, a visit encouraged by letters he had received from his Aunt Lucy asking him if he was 'Harry's boy, who'd made good'. The letters also contained an invitation to visit the side of the family that had remained in Britain when Bob had left for America with his mother and brothers to join his father in Cleveland, and to meet his grandfather, now ninety-six.

It was too good an opportunity to miss, and both Bob and Dolores were excited at the prospect as they fitted in a number of vaudeville engagements before embarking on the *Normandie* in New York. They played Minneapolis, Chicago and Atlantic City, enjoyed a reunion on the way with Bob's relatives in Cleveland, and then moved into a ten-day engagement at the Paramount in New York. All were highly successful for the touring group which, in addition to Bob and Dolores, included Jerry Colonna, the zany comedian with the popping eyes, walrus moustache and piercing voice, who had become a regular member of Hope's radio show.

The vacation was high on nostalgia. Bob took Dolores to see 44 Craigton Road, Eltham, where he was born, and they spent a couple of days in Hitchin, where his family joined them for a big reunion party. Bob was proud of the progress he had made in show business so far, but the frank comments of his relatives were calculated to keep his feet firmly on the ground. It took him a long time to find a relative who had seen even one of his pictures.

The vacation had started out in style. The 1930s were the glamour days of Atlantic crossings by luxury ocean liner and, in spite of the gathering war clouds in Europe, the quayside send-off was traditionally exciting with hooters blasting, farewells shouted, streamers and whistles. Adding to the general confusion and disarray were an estimated 500 autograph-hunters who screamed for the signatures of a small army of embarking movie idols which included Charles Boyer, George Raft, Edward G. Robinson, Madeleine Carroll and Ben Lyon and Bebe Daniels. (The latter were to become favourites with British radio audiences.) The atmosphere was festive, celebratory, buoyant, through a now bubbling American economy which had survived the dark, perilous days of the Wall Street Crash and had not only reached the light at the end of the tunnel but had emerged into the brilliant sunshine of a booming economy.

The return voyage was in stark contrast. After spending time in Britain, Bob and Dolores had caught the boat train to France, but the enchantment of Paris was stifled for them by the threat of war. It was a threat which Bob had not taken seriously. Before leaving America and when questioned a couple of times by Dolores on board ship and in Europe, he had stated his conviction that war would not come, but now — in the third week of August 1939 — he had to acknowledge the looming danger. Their accommodation on the *Queen Mary* was for the mid September sailing, but urged by pleas from Paramount and NBC executives to get back as soon as possible, they cut short their holiday and managed to book on the previous sailing, leaving Britain on a much overcrowded *Queen Mary* on 30 August. Two days later five powerful German armies were ordered into Poland by Hitler. British Prime Minister Neville Chamberlain declared war on Germany two days later, on Sunday, 3 September, after Hitler had not responded to an ultimatum.

The mood on board ship was sombre and portentous. There was fear and anxiety for friends and, in Bob's case, family also, left behind. There was also apprehension lest the luxury liner become the immediate target for German U-boats. Dolores brought the news of war to Bob when she returned to their cabin after attending Mass. His natural instinct about the scheduled ship's concert that night was to cancel, but against his judgement the captain persuaded him to go through with it, on the basis that comedy and music were exactly what the passengers needed.

After entertaining the passengers for an hour with his normal vaudeville routine, Bob went into a special version of his theme song, a parody he had written himself:

> Thanks for the memory
> Of this great ocean trip
> On England's finest ship.
> Tho' they packed them to the rafters,
> They never made a slip.
> Ah! Thank you so much.

61

Then into the second verse:

> Thanks for the memory.
> Some folks slept on the floor,
> Some in the corridor,
> But I was more exclusive,
> My room had 'Gentlemen' above the door.
> Ah! Thank you so much.

The passengers roared their approval and on arrival in New York were each given a copy, printed by the ship's press.

With the vacation abruptly ended, Bob found himself facing a terrifyingly heavy programme in both radio and pictures. But before that, he and Dolores shared in a precious moment when Dolores received a call from 'The Cradle' at Evanston, Illinois. For some time they had known they could not have children and had now agreed to adopt, though Bob had questioned the idea at first. 'The Cradle' had been recommended to them by George and Gracie Burns, as one of the country's most distinguished adoption homes, and the long and tedious business of being accepted as possible parents had been started some time before they had left for Europe. Now Dolores travelled from California to Evanston and returned to Bob with Linda Theresa, their new baby, the first of their four adopted children.

A second season of Pepsodent-sponsored NBC broadcasts made Bob one of America's top radio comedians, with none other than Judy Garland brought in at a hefty fee as his regular co-star.

Meantime, over at Paramount they were dusting down a script called *The Road to Mandalay,* adapted by scriptwriters Frank Butler and Don Hartman from a South Seas story called *Beach of Dreams* by Harry Hervey.

Why this particular story was being examined is perhaps as difficult to pin-point as is the person who might claim the credit for bringing Hope, Crosby and Lamour together. When contemplating the first part of the puzzle it is as well to remember that Hollywood was producing hundreds of pictures a year at that time and was picking up stories from almost anywhere it could find them and getting writers to adapt them for the big screen. In 1939 and 1940 Paramount alone released more than 110 movies, a conveyor-belt output averaging more than two every week. It was a demanding schedule.

As to the second part of the puzzle, it is impossible to ignore the role of Paramount's production chief, William LeBaron. He spent little more than a couple of years with Paramount, but that was more than long enough to bring together one of the cinema's classic comedy teams of all time.

Widespread belief has it that LeBaron originally wanted Fred MacMurray and Jack Oakie for the picture. When they turned him down, he then wanted Burns and Allen, but they were not available. His thoughts now diverted to the professional leg-pulling which was going on between Bing Crosby and Bob Hope, and the way in which they good-naturedly insulted each other at every opportunity — especially at Bing's Del Mar Turf Club.

The 'vendetta' had started when Hope guestéd on Crosby's Kraft radio show more than a year before and, with Bob carrying it on every time he went on the air, it was attracting an impressive following, proving a good money-spinner and helping to promote their reputations as quick-witted, slick, up-to-the-minute professional humorists. What should be more natural than that LeBaron should now choose them for the new picture? Or that sarong girl Dorothy Lamour should be brought in to complete the tropical island flavour once the film had been re-titled *Road to Singapore*?

Lamour has a somewhat different story of how it happened. She recalls that she had just finished lunch one day at the Paramount Studios and was on her way out when she stopped at a table shared by Bob and Bing, evidently in fine form, cracking jokes and spiking each other. Dorothy was still laughing when she came across two writer friends from the Paramount team. 'What's so funny?' they asked. In her book *My Side of the Road,* she explains what happened next: 'I told them that I had just been joking with Hope and Crosby and that if they could only come up with a story involving two crazy guys and a "gal in the middle" I would love to play her.' Dorothy goes on to say that these two writers have forgotten the brief conversation she says took place that day — she also claims that Oakie and MacMurray do not recall being offered *Road to Singapore* parts — but she says that soon after, the first *Road* story was turned in to the front office and she got her wish to star in it with Hope and Crosby.

What is without dispute is that the picture was seen as only a one-off comedy musical. That there could be a follow-up or a series of pictures was not contemplated when *Road to Singapore* was being made. By all accounts, making the picture was a riot and a constant hazard for the director and technicians who were responsible for maintaining some sanity and order amid the incessant tomfoolery of Bob and Bing. There was a natural rapport between the two, and their ad-libbing knew few bounds.

At the start Lamour, who was a polished professional who used to learn her lines thoroughly for every film, thought that *Road to Singapore* was no different from any other film. When she arrived on the first day Bob and Bing were doing a scene, and she sat and watched. Then she realized that nothing in the dialogue sounded familiar. It wasn't at all like the script she had read. She thought perhaps there had been some extensive re-writes, but when she did her first scene with the two of them she learned the worst. Bob and Bing had been making it up as they went along. Their ability to extemporize with rapid responses often took the script well off course, and in that first scene Dorothy kept waiting for her cue, but it never came. Exasperated and frustrated, she finally broke in. 'Please, guys, when can I get my line in?' Lamour says they both stopped dead, broke up and laughed for ten minutes.

In movie-making Dorothy Lamour was more experienced than either of her co-stars. She had a sultry, sensual attraction and a beautiful figure, shown to perfection in the sarong-clad roles in the South Sea island movies in which she had until then specialized. To Hope and Crosby all this meant nothing. They had known each other for some time and they ribbed her mercilessly. Fortunately she had a sharp sense of fun and was a true professional.

'After the first few days I decided that it was ridiculous to waste time learning the script. I would read over the next day's work only to get the idea of what was happening,' said Lamour. 'What I really needed was a good night's sleep to be in shape for the next morning's ad-libs. This method provided some very interesting results on the screen. In fact I used to ask to see the finished rushes just to see what the movie was all about.'

No feature film had ever been made with such a degree of spontaneity, nor perhaps with such accompanying arrogance on the part of the perpetrators. Their good-natured innocence didn't always make up for what they were doing, certainly for writers Don Hartman and Frank Butler. It didn't soothe their anger at having their words so wholeheartedly tampered with to hear Hope call out on one occasion: 'Hey, Don, if you recognize any of yours, yell "Bingo!"' It's not surprising he stormed out to complain to LeBaron.

The picture has a simple plot. Ace Lannigan (Bob) wants to get away from an old girl friend. The father of Josh Mallon (Bing) plans for him to marry and take over the family steamship line. At Bing's engagement party the pair decide to opt out, and they end up in exotic Kaigoon in the South Seas where they meet a beautiful dancer called Mima (Dorothy) and her infamous partner and enforced minder, Caesar (played by 'bad guy' Anthony Quinn). After that the plot is virtually immaterial.

Jerry Colonna was also worked into the cast list, along with Charles Coburn, Judith Barrett and Johnny Arthur.

The film is also remembered for its songs. Bing's subsequent record of 'Sweet Potato Piper' became quite a big seller. Others were 'Too Romantic', 'Kaigoon' and 'The Moon and the Willow Tree'.

What was to become the famous Hope-Crosby 'pattercake' routine had its first public showing in *Road to Singapore*. Threatened by Tony Quinn, they stop what they are doing, bend down and begin playing the old children's game of 'Pattercake, pattercake, baker's man', touching their knees and each other's hands in rhythm. Quinn doesn't know what is going on and is puzzled by this quick turn of events. While he is off guard, our heroes have the chance to flatten him and run. It became a *Road* standby, a classic comedy cameo of the time and a trademark.

Bob and Bing's abuse of the script was one thing, their off-camera frolics another, and not always as easily tolerated. It is not difficult to understand, for instance, that their fooling had gone too far when the special soapsuds which the effects department had provided for Lamour (for washing Bob and Bing's clothes in an old-fashioned washtub) were used by Bob for throwing at Bing and Dorothy during a lunch break. Then Bing moved in, and he and Bob began hurling the suds at Dorothy. This led to a chase around the studio set, across the sound stage and surrounding areas, and finished up with Lamour chasing the pair of them into a crowded dining-room and dumping a huge can of suds over their heads.

It seems that Bob had been the instigator, with that predisposition to the practical joke which he had displayed strongly enough with Shirley Ross in *Thanks for the Memory*. The director of that film, George Archainbaud, didn't much like the way Hope, used to working before an audience, would test his jokes on the stage crew, gagging his way through rehearsals. Archainbaud was also irritated by the way Bob and Shirley chewed gum incessantly, supposedly to relax and to keep their breath fresh. They continued chewing through rehearsals, which gave problems of movement when cameras were being focused. This led to a row, and the situation lost all proportion as it was rumoured on the set that Bob and Shirley intended to sing and chew at the same time during their ballad 'Two Sleepy People'. The expectancy built up to such a pitch that technicians and other workers from nearby units filtered onto the Hope-Ross set to see what could have been one almighty bust-up. Bob kept the situation bubbling during rehearsal, but once Archainbaud announced a take and the cameras started to roll, he and Shirley did what they had always intended to do as professionals: they took the gum from their mouths and stuck it under their chairs. Then, as the tension eased away and the music started, Bob is alleged to have said: 'I thought we'd draw a better house than this — most of these are in on passes.' How was any director supposed to cope with a character like this?

Bob, Bing and Dorothy had enormous fun making *Road to Singapore* and though, when shooting was over, the crew packed their bags with some relief, it is said that they tried hard to be chosen for another *Road* picture because of the atmosphere, fun and sheer talent of Hope and Crosby.

Bob said afterwards: 'The *Road* pictures had the excitement of a live entertainment, not a movie set. Some stars banned visitors on the set, but Bing and I liked to have people around.'

Some of the credit for the success of *Road to Singapore,* and of the *Road* pictures still to come, should be handed to Bob's gag-writers. He got into the habit of giving a new script to his writers so that they could work on suitable jokes to 'punch up' scenes in the picture.

The sensitivity of director Vic Schertzinger, and his common-sense handling of the Hope-Crosby way of working their films together, should not be overlooked. In the midst of the turmoil, he had done well to maintain any semblance of order. At first irritated and impatient with the free-wheeling attitude of Hope and Crosby and the extent of their ad-libbing, he was sharp enough to detect that, for all their lack of discipline — or maybe because of it, what was coming out in the rushes was fresh, vivid, spontaneous and, most important of all, likely to make good box office.

Bob said Schertzinger was the ideal director for their kind of technique. He cited one case where he and Bing, along with Dorothy, had been tossing the jokes and insults back and forth for close on five minutes, building up an exceptional atmosphere and pace. Although Schertzinger had realized that Hope had stepped into shadow momentarily towards the end of the sequence, which would normally have meant a re-take, he surprisingly wrapped the scene. When what looked to others like an oversight was pointed out to him by his assistant, it made no difference. A re-take could not possibly have captured the sparkle and spirit of the original, he said, and the scene stayed.

Pandemonium the making of Road to Singapore might have been by generally accepted standards, it was nevertheless more structured and defined in terms of plot than the epics which followed. It was also different from its successors in that audiences were led to believe that Hope wins Lamour, while Crosby goes back to his father and snobbish fiancée. But then, almost as a postscript, it transpires that Hope doesn't marry Lamour after all, and when Bob and Bing meet by chance at the end of the picture, Bob admits to Bing that the latter is the guy Lamour really wants. Thereafter Bing used to get the girl.

But that title — why *Road to Singapore*? And where does Singapore figure in the story? That was another gimmick, to be used for the *Road* pictures that followed. They never did reach Singapore — or Zanzibar, Bali, Morocco or their other destinations in any of the *Road* films suggested by the titles. In the case of *Road to Singapore,* they set out with the firm intention of getting there but progressed no further after landing on the mythical tropical paradise of Kaigoon.

Paramount chiefs were glad to see the end of filming on *Road to Singapore.* At that time, of course, they had no indication of the box-office bonanza it would turn out to be, and in any event they urgently wanted Hope so they could team him again with Paulette Goddard to capitalize on the triumph of their first film together, *The Cat and the Canary.* So successful were Paramount in producing a near-carbon copy sequel that, uncharitably, you could say that any discernible difference between the two pictures was purely coincidental.

For this latest effort Paramount went right back to the early 1900s and dusted off an old Broadway play by Paul Dickey and Charles Goddard which pre-dated the first 1914 film version which featured H.B. Warner. It was remade in 1922 with Wallace Reid and Lila Lee in the starring roles, and brought out again for Hope and Goddard after Walter DeLeon had given a new polish to the screenplay. The haunted-house framework was retained and Hope, as a wise-cracking cowardly hero, is called on, as Paramount's own story by John Douglas Eames so succinctly puts it, 'to help Goddard claim her inheritance and survive clutching hands, shrieks in the night, voodoo curses and his jokes in a Cuban mansion of horrors'.

The film, *The Ghost Breakers,* was produced by Arthur Hornblow Jr, who had also produced *The Cat and the Canary,* and the director was George Marshall, a film-maker of great tradition who had worked on Tom Mix Westerns before specializing in comedy.

Though the picture was a blatant attempt to cash in on the earlier success, the public appeared not to worry about such things. They enjoyed seeing Bob Hope and Paulette Goddard on screen together again, enthused over the combination of classic melodramatic horror and a heavy coating of obvious comedy, and couldn't find their way to the box office fast enough. It was another big hit, and Bob Hope was now a major movie star to be reckoned with, for *Road to Singapore* was already putting the broadest of smiles on the faces of the studio bosses at Paramount.

In a sense, Bob had suddenly become a problem. *Singapore* was released on 22 March, 1940, and *The Ghost Breakers* just three months later. Both were soon doing good enough business for urgent sequels to be called for, but *Singapore* was in the lead and was to go on to make a magnificent profit for Paramount of around $1.5 million. Bob Hope had a lot going for him at this point and was always more than willing to drop the comedy lines when it came to talking money for his contracts, particularly when he was in a strong position to negotiate a good deal. He was now a big name on radio, in demand for personal appearances and as master of ceremonies for the Oscar Awards and other important and prestigious occasions, and showed himself to be more than happy to pick up the choice dates in vaudeville whenever he fancied a tour.

Bob also knew how the big studios would sign actors and actresses to term contracts at a fee and were then in a position to maintain their pay at that level long after their success in terms of revenue to the studio would suggest a salary level four, five or even six times higher. He didn't intend to be caught in that trap. He figured that, with Paramount clamouring for him to do another *Road* picture right away with Crosby and Lamour, the timing to stake his claim for a pay rise couldn't be better.

He was however, immediately committed to a five-week tour with his radio show, interspersed with personal appearances, and the response to these proved to be enormous. Massive crowds turned out, and in Chicago the queues were so long that he completed as many as seven shows in one single day. His fee and share of box-office receipts soared to more than $30,000 in just one week. Bolstered by this success he told his agent, Louie Shurr, to go to Paramount and tell them that his price for a picture must now be: $50,000.

The shrewd 'Doc' did better than that. He had already spoken to Paramount studio boss Y. Frank Freeman, who was insisting that Hope fulfil his current contract at the previously agreed fee. He also knew that the great film-maker Sam Goldwyn desperately wanted Bob to do a picture with him, so he traded one off against the other. If he couldn't get the extra cash from Paramount, he would get it from Goldwyn. He knew that Freeman, having recently borrowed Gary Cooper from Goldwyn for a picture at Paramount, would feel under an obligation to return the favour, so agreed that Hope would complete his remaining option of four pictures on the original terms, on condition that Freeman loan him out for a Goldwyn picture. He agreed.

Now started the hard battle with Goldwyn over money. Shurr and his tough-bargaining partner, Al Melnick, went to see Goldwyn in his office. Sam opened with pleasantries, saying how much he admired Hope and how eager he was to make a picture with him.

'But, Mr Goldwyn, we haven't talked money,' said Shurr.

'Don't worry about money,' said Sam. 'I'll give him anything he wants.'

Melnick seized his opportunity. 'Bob Hope wants a hundred thousand.'

'Forget it,' said Goldwyn. 'Our conversation is over.'

For a time it seemed that the gamble had failed, but Bob was determined to stick it out, and it was he in the end who pushed the deal through, taking advantage of a series of Texas premières of the Gary Cooper movie *The Westerner,* and at which he was helping Goldwyn out. The premières had gone well, and Sam was in a good mood. Just before the start of the last show, 'I'd like to get an agreement on what you're going to pay me for the movie,' Bob told Goldwyn. Sam put him off, saying they would talk about it later, but Bob wasn't put off and quickly hit on a plan.

When it was time for Bob to introduce Goldwyn to the audience, he gave him such a build-up that Sam came on stage so delighted that he not only thanked Bob for his generous introduction but went on to explain how he hadn't done a comedy picture since the days of Eddie Cantor because he never found a comedian who could do as well — until now: Bob Hope. Hope came back quickly. In a remarkable ploy, he announced through the microphone: 'That's very nice, Sam, but let's talk money.'

Taken off guard, Goldwyn responded: 'Not now, Bob. Later.' But Bob didn't intend letting him off the hook. 'Not later. Now. These folk won't mind.'

He then invited Sam to get a little more comfortable and, grabbing the microphone, lay down on the stage, inviting Goldwyn to join him. With little option the legendary moviemaker did just that, and although numerous accounts of the incident do not reveal whether Bob was eventually paid the sum he was after, he relates the ending of this astonishing exchange like this: 'The audience roared as Sam got down on the stage with me. We conversed about my salary, then I got up and announced: "Folks, it will be a great pleasure for me to make a picture for Mr Goldwyn." The audience was screaming and a *Life* photographer came out and shot the bizarre sight.' Bob reported that Goldwyn later ordered the pictures to be 'killed'.

Having been the unfortunate victim of such a public demonstration, it is surprising that Goldwyn ever spoke to Bob Hope again, let alone allowed him to go ahead with the starring role in one of his major pictures. It says much for his character and his own sense of humour and fun that he did — and perhaps something about Bob Hope's wholesome and captivating professionalism, with its absence of vindictiveness, not only that he had the audacity to contemplate such a trick but that his reputation, and the respect he enjoyed with his public and his peers, was sufficient for him to pull it off without blemishing his image. Its freakish quality puts the whole incident down as being well worthy of inclusion in any of the zany *Road* pictures.

Bob did just two movies for Goldwyn. *They Got Me Covered* was released in 1943. *The Princess and the Pirate* came out in 1944. In the first he appeared with his Paramount co-star Dorothy Lamour, also borrowed by Goldwyn for the picture, and in the second he was with the blonde and beautiful Virginia Mayo in the early days of her film career.

In *They Got Me Covered* Bob plays the part of a foreign correspondent trying to regain his job after being fired for missing the story of Germany's invasion of Russia. In trying to make amends he becomes entangled with fugitives and spies but ends up a hero, solving all the problems and capturing all the bad guys on his own.

In *The Princess and the Pirate,* Bob is 'Sylvester the Great', an eighteenth-century wandering magician of sorts who turns spoof swashbuckling hero while on his way to America. On board ship with Virginia Mayo, who is really a princess travelling incognito, fleeing from her father who won't let her marry a commoner, he somehow manages to survive mutinies, treasure hunts and sea battles, with the old film 'heavy' Victor McLaglen leading a bunch of villainous cut-throats.

In most analyses of Bob Hope's career in pictures, these two Goldwyn features receive scant attention. Against the much more dominantly successful *Road* pictures, they admittedly offer limited impact, but that's not to say that they do not have their moments.

Two sequences from *The Princess and the Pirate* will strike the right chord with most Hope buffs. As Sylvester, the man of many faces, he takes off his make-up and goes to remove his putty nose, only to find that it is his own. Then, towards the end of the film, he thinks he is all set to take Mayo in his arms — and after the hazards they have been through together, who can say he doesn't deserve her? — but Virginia prefers an ordinary seaman — who turns out to be Crosby. In disgust Hope asserts: 'This is the last picture I make for Goldwyn.'

When Bob returned to Paramount to honour his contract commitments, he was teamed with Bing Crosby and Dorothy Lamour for the second *Road,* which this time saw them setting off for Zanzibar.

Meantime on radio his surging reputation was boosted by the decision to take his *Pepsodent Show* to the airmen at the March Field army air base some seventy miles outside Hollywood — the start of his almost obsessive entertaining of service personnel, which was to continue for some fifteen years. It brought him recognition richly deserved. He was voted the top comedian of the nation and was named top radio star, ahead of Bing Crosby and Jack Benny.

Soon, as the United States edged ever closer to war, though no one realized it at the time, Bob Hope was also counted among the biggest box-office draws in the movie industry, along with such superstars as Mickey Rooney, Clark Gable, Spencer Tracy, James Cagney, Bette Davis, Judy Garland and Gary Cooper. It was reported openly that his gross income for 1940, from pictures, radio and personal appearances, topped $460,000.

It was a frantically hectic life, but Bob and Dolores managed to find the time to celebrate their daughter Linda's first birthday by welcoming their second child from the same home in Evanston. They christened their new baby son Tony.

5 Firmly on the Road

In 1935 Bing Crosby had been in Hollywood for several years and was already a big star, but that year he returned briefly to New York for a personal appearance, and Bob took him out to Ben Marden's Riviera Club in New Jersey, where Harry Richman and Sophie Tucker were in the show. On their way back that night, crossing the George Washington Bridge, Bing said to Bob: 'If you ever decide to come to California, let me know. Maybe we can get together on something.'

It is unlikely that Bob ever reminded Bing of his remark. Nor did Bing ever claim any kind of credit for bringing them together as a team. But *Road to Singapore,* their first film as co-stars, became the kind of 'something' which extended wildly beyond their imaginations those several years before on the George Washington Bridge. Paramount made the picture as a medium-budget pot-boiler, and its enormous financial success produced an unexpected pot of gold for a studio desperately in need of cash.

The years of Depression in the early 1930s had brought hard times to film makers. Paramount had slumped into receivership and, though fortunes brightened in 1935 and 1936 with profits up to $3 million and $6 million respectively, they had fallen below $3 million again in 1938-9. Bolstered by the runaway success of *Singapore,* it's not surprising that the studio bosses rushed through a sequel.

Singapore's writers, Don Hartman and Frank Butler, were commissioned for the new screenplay, and Victor Schertzinger again directed. The story was taken from a Don Hartman original called *Find Colonel Fawcett* and featured Bob and Bing as a couple of carnival con-men let loose in darkest Africa. Paramount wisely stayed close to *Singapore*'s winning formula, but this time had Bing (as Chuck Reardon) and Bob (as Fearless Frazier) getting involved with Dorothy Lamour (as Donna

Latour!) and Una Merkel, playing stranded performers trying to scrounge enough money to get themselves back to civilization. They persuade Bing and Bob to take them along with them, and their sequence of highly improbable adventures together is what the film is all about. It includes cannibals, wild animals, Bing gambling his money on a phoney diamond mine and Bob being conned into saving Lamour from 'white slavery' and grappling with a gorilla.

Aficionados of Hope-Crosby-Lamour films usually agree that the yet-to-come *Road to Morocco* was the best of the entire *Road* series, but they are equally in accord that the second film in the series, *Road to Zanzibar,* was better than *Singapore.*

In a sense the first picture emerged instinctively. This was due to the influence Hope and Crosby, as performers and through their gag-writers, had on the detail and structure of the script, and also because director Schertzinger was able to identify and appreciate the value of the spontaneity which it brought. *Zanzibar* benefited from their being able to work from the new, previously uncharted baseline established by *Singapore* and to move forward from that point. In practical terms, it meant that the characterization of Bob and Bing was more firmly established in *Zanzibar.* Crosby became the adventurer, the schemer, the instigator, and the successful wooer, however teasingly long delayed, of Dorothy Lamour. Hope became the trusting follower, destined to lose and be victimized, frustrated by his enthusiastic but adolescent attempts to win the girl, impish and overbearing, yet ingratiating and agreeable.

The picture is also notable for the assumption it makes that audiences would have seen *Road to Singapore.* This novel technique is tentative in *Zanzibar.* Facing the villain, the boys swing into their pattercake routine, but this time he slugs them before they have chance to reach the pay-off action. Sprawled ruefully on the floor, Bob cracks to the camera: 'He must have seen the picture.' This technique was to be used increasingly as the *Road* series developed. It also began to absorb references and hints to non-*Road* films Hope and Crosby had been in, and even to their respective lives outside movies, in golf and their radio series, and Dorothy Lamour's public image as a sarong-clad beauty to be found on those romantic South Sea islands.

The improbable tone of the film is set in the first sequences. The carnival location presents Hope as 'The Living Bullet', a human cannon-ball, with Crosby pulling in the fairground crowds with the song 'You Lucky People, You'. Things go wrong when a dummy (not Bob) is fired from the cannon, through a hoop of fire, hits a circus tent, starts a fire and destroys everything. Bing and Bob are already fleeing as the circus-owner and his gang give chase.

Zanzibar is generally reckoned funnier than *Singapore,* and commercially the team scored another amazing hit. Profits once again soared beyond the $1 million mark. The film's songs — 'You Lucky People, You', 'Road to Zanzibar', 'You're Dangerous' and 'It's Always You' — are pleasant and easy to listen to, though perhaps for the first time in a Bob Hope picture, there was not a song which was particularly memorable.

Again there seems to have been almost as much fun on the set as in the picture, and a good deal more chaos. Lamour continued to find Hope and Crosby a handful, though now, with her experience of working with them on *Singapore,* she beats them occasionally at their own game. Dotty recalls one particular incident. She explains that during one rehearsal she remained very tight-lipped while Bob and Bing were giving her a hard time. The scene ended with them both turning to her and saying, 'How about it?' and waiting expectantly for her response. Says Dotty: 'I smiled demurely and they fell on their faces. Make-up man Harry Ray had blacked out two of my front teeth.'

She explains how, on another occasion, a flu epidemic hit the set and they made a sign with the names of Hope, Crosby, Lamour, Merkel and Schertzinger on it, on which current temperatures were posted by the side of the names — the one with the lowest temperature had to buy lunch. Bob lost out in that particular prank.

Hollywood alone was now keeping Bob busy. Three more pictures of his were completed and released in 1941 — *Caught in the Draft* on 4 July, *Nothing but the Truth* on 10 October, and *Louisiana Purchase* on 25 December. The response to the two *Road* films had guaranteed that there would be more offerings of a similar kind, so long as the paying customers continued to roll up at the box offices in their millions, but Bob's remaining pictures in 1941 were also significant because they gave him the first opportunity to exercise and develop his talent for a wider range of comedy.

After only two *Road* films, Bob and Bing, with Dotty, had

already done enough to qualify them for acceptance into the exclusive club of top comedy teams. Before the *Roads* Bob had shown his worth in handling, as writer Bob Thomas classified them, character comedies and comedy adventure. The remaining pictures of 1941, again according to Bob Thomas, allowed him to demonstrate his talent for handling farce.

Caught in the Draft teamed Bob yet again with Dorothy Lamour, other notables in the cast list being Lynne Overman and Eddie Bracken. It was noted for its topicality and was another major hit for Hope, Lamour and the studio, but it cannot rate with the *Road* films in terms of historical significance.

Bob is cast as a Hollywood star who reluctantly joins the army and ends up confounding and exasperating the colonel — and marrying his daughter (Miss Lamour). Overman takes the part of Bob's agent, and Bracken, who incidentally was at one time earning money writing gags for Bob, is cast in the role of his chauffeur. Both join up with Bob and are assigned to the same training camp.

The idea came from producer Buddy DeSylva, who wanted to capture the spirit of the times as the first Americans were being drafted. He had Harry Tugend write an original story and screenplay and, according to Bob, Paramount gave him the part to see how good an actor he was. Even if that had been true — and it wasn't! — Bob didn't let them down, for he measured up well to the demands of the film under the skilful direction of David Butler, whom he admired greatly.

In *Nothing but the Truth* Bob is teamed for the third time with Paulette Goddard. For the reunion, producer Arthur Hornblow Jr chose an updated version of a 1916 Broadway play which had already been filmed successfully twice before. Don Hartman and Ken Englund were brought in to write this latest account of the James Montgomery original adapted from a novel by Frederic S. Isham. Fun and farce abound as Bob (as stockbroker Steve Bennett tries to tell only the truth for twenty-four hours to win a $10,000 bet with colleagues.

In a sense this third-time pairing of Bob Hope with Paulette Goddard reflected the doubts of the studio bosses at that time. They didn't know in 1940 that the *Road* films were going to be such a phenomenal success and were watching for any box-office possibilities in teaming Hope with Goddard. *The Cat and the Canary* and *The Ghost Breakers* had both shown such good profits through the box office that it wasn't until the enormous success of *Singapore* and then *Zanzibar* that Paramount were prepared to relinquish whatever potential the Hope-Goddard partnership might have held, in favour of building the *Roads* into a series.

Paramount was never known for an all-out policy of presenting musicals with the dedication and drive of MGM, and in the 1940s their new-found fortune resulted from a blend of comedies, war films, melodramas and musicals. Their film version of Irving Berlin's musical hit on Broadway, *Louisiana Purchase*, included Bob (as Jim Taylor) working with Vera Zorina, Victor Moore and Irene Bordoni. The film stuck close to the stage presentation and was boosted at the box office by being shot in Technicolor. The plot has Bob framed by associates of the Louisiana Purchasing Company and under investigation by US Senator Oliver P. Loganberry (played by Victor Moore). The associates then force Bob to lead the Senator into compromising situations with Zorina and Bordoni. Among a number of enjoyable musical numbers, the theme song, 'Louisiana Purchase', was popular for a time, but 'It's a Lovely Day Tomorrow' was the tune which became a major hit of the day and was to last as an Irving Berlin standard.

Just eighteen days before the official release of *Louisiana Purchase*, the United States was thrust into war through the unprovoked attack by the Japanese on Pearl Harbor on 7 December, 1941. Aside from the stark horror of the attack and the heavy casualties sustained by the Americans, Bob Hope may well have felt some release of tension and unease that America was now openly in the battle for freedom. No one could say that he was not a hundred per cent American — he had become an American citizen as long before as 1920, along with his brothers and parents — but his loyalty towards the country of his birth was exceptional for someone who had been away so long. It satisfied his dual patriotism to have America standing openly beside Britain in the ultimate fight for freedom.

The obsession Bob was to develop for entertaining fighting men and women, which was to continue for something like thirty-five years, had its origins about this time. Of course, as an entertainer he was not alone in taking off on long, arduous and at times difficult and dangerous tours to entertain troops, but he did seem to take on more of them than most Hollywood stars.

It was also about this time that he began making professional visits to Britain and the continent of Europe. Bob was already a massive radio star in the United States and his following in the UK was also legion, enthusiastic and dedicated. His schedule of radio work, personal appearances, morale-boosting tours and film-making in the early to mid-1940s was prodigious.

In 1943 Bob returned to London at the start of an extensive tour of Britain, North Africa and the Mediterranean. Though the Blitz, which had caused him so much concern for the old country, was well over, the tour brought him close to wartime action for the first time. In Sicily, while entertaining a 19,000 uniformed audience, he joined everyone else in darting for cover as the Luftwaffe sprang a surprise raid. Back in London he met wartime leader Winston Churchill, entertained Allied service-men and women at the Odeon in Leicester Square and boosted war-torn morale with a constant stream of gags — and simply by being there.

It was the only wartime visit Bob made to Britain, but coinciden-tally he was back shortly after peace in Europe was declared in May 1945. His appearance at the Royal Albert Hall was a sell-out, with disappointed queues outside unable to gain entry.

It was late 1946, meanwhile, when Bob and Dolores went back to Evanston to collect another baby, this time a two-month-old girl. There was also a three-month-old boy available for adoption, and Dolores was very tempted. She was about to talk to Bob about having both babies when he turned to her and said: 'I've already signed for them both. I couldn't bear to think about leaving him behind.'

Back in London in November 1947, he compèred an impor-tant gala stage show, broadcast his famous *Pepsodent Show,* watched the royal wedding procession of the Duke of Edinburgh and Princess Elizabeth from a privileged position overlooking the Mall, and presented the King with a commemorative book of photographs autographed by 400 of Hollywood's most success-ful and brightest stars. According to Charles Thompson in his excellent biography of Hope, *The Road from Eltham,* the King and Queen immediately thumbed through the book and together enquired: 'Where's Bing Crosby's portrait?' Bob found it hurriedly for them. 'Here it is,' he said, adding 'and he signed it with his middle name — three crosses.'

The following year he was back for a Royal Command Performance at the London Palladium in front of King George VI. In a sense these excursions to Britain were preliminary skirmishes in preparation for his major impact in the 1950s and beyond. For British fans that decade was probably the peak of his popularity. He became a frequent visitor, appearing at the world-famous London Palladium when that historic theatre was perhaps at the pinnacle of its acclaim as the home of variety, and in Royal Variety Performances. This concentration of British activity began in April 1951, when his two-week season at the Prince of Wales Theatre brought enthusiastic Press notices.

By that time Bob had been accepted as one of the world's greatest entertainers. His impact on radio alone was enormous and as a cinema celebrity he was basking in the glory of having made no fewer than twenty major films since *Road to Zanzibar*, including three more phenomenally successful *Road* pictures. His stay at the Prince of Wales was a sell-out, as was his special gala concert at the London Palladium on Sunday, 29 April, 1951.

Bob's work schedule was of marathon proportions, but in the middle of more filming, more radio work, more personal appearances, long tours and a good deal of charity work, those legendary impresarios Val Parnell and Lew Grade managed to bring him back to Britain the very next year, 1952, for a two-week engagement at the Palladium, which broke all box-office records. These were the days of the Skyrockets Orchestra and the famous Palladium Tiller Girls. Also on the bill were Frances Duncan (aerialist), Clifford Stanton ('Personalities on Parade'), Fred Sanborn (the speechless comic), Vic and Adio (two boys from Brazil) and, billed as England's 'three little sisters', the Beverley Sisters. Bob's act had the support of Betsy Duncan and Jerry Desmonde, one-time stooge for the great British comedian Sid Field, for whom Bob had the greatest respect.

Thirty-five years later, as I sat with the Beverley Sisters in their brand-new north London home (two years after their astonishingly successful come-back to show business), they remembered the happy times they had spent with Hope during many appearances together, and particularly at the Palladium back in 1952.

They recalled instantly an experience from the very first day's rehearsal of that 1952 Palladium show which, they said, endeared him to them for ever.

Babs told the story: 'There was something wrong with our

band parts and I wanted to make a tiny alteration and began looking for an eraser. I couldn't find one, so I shouted out: "Has anybody got a rubber?" Everybody started laughing and we didn't know why. So I shouted louder: "Surely somebody's got a rubber?"'

Teddie butted in to remind me that they were very young at the time. Then Babs went on: 'We simply didn't know what was going on, as Bob's entourage and then virtually everyone around us broke into gales of laughter. Innocently, I led us further into trouble when I said something like . . . "Bob Hope, he's the richest man here, he's got to have a rubber."'

The sisters agreed that the situation was by then getting a little out of hand and they knew that it was obviously all at their expense.

Babs went on: 'And do you know, that darling man suddenly said why didn't we all have a break, and he came over and said: "Let's go and have some coffee. We're having fun." He took us down to the stalls and we had coffee and he said: "I didn't like you being laughed at, to be the only ones not in on the joke" and then went on to explain about the differences in the American language and what a rubber meant in America.

'We thought it was marvellous that the most important man there didn't want us to be laughed at — you see, we were too young for somebody to yell out to us across the stage what it was all about. But you would have thought that, as a comedian, he would have laughed and been rough about it and let it go, but instead he thought about us.'

The Bevs agreed that, if he had said 'condom', they wouldn't have understood in those days anyway; if they'd known about such things at all, it was by another name entirely!

They loved him for the way he looked after them but admitted that on other occasions, with more worldly and experienced people, he could drive his joking hard. They recalled a time at the Palladium when Bob leg-pulled the famous Lew Grade unmercifully. It was before he became a lord, but he was still an intimidating figure and, because of his enormous stature and influence within show business, was generally looked upon with awe by almost everyone.

Bob's act included a sequence where a waiter came on with a tray with medicine on it. He would take the medicine and jump up and down to shake it, and the waiter would walk off. It was the last night of the season and when the waiter came on, it wasn't the waiter at all but, of all people, Lew Grade. The Bevs explained that he did everything he should have done but then Bob announced: 'Ladies and Gentlemen — you may think this is a waiter standing here, but he was once the Charleston Champion of the world,' and without hesitation he got bandleader Wolfe Phillips to play some Charleston music and urged Lew to do a few demonstration steps.

The girls said it was all completely spontaneous and they were standing in the wings killing themselves with laughter as Bob made Lew suffer, urging him on, telling the orchestra to continue playing and inciting the audience to clap and keep the joke going.

The telling of one memory sparked off another. The girls agreed that Bob's singing voice was much under-rated. Said Joy: 'We would be sitting in the dressing-room getting ready to go on when the sound of his singing would come over the tannoy, a sensitive song — "Invitation to a Dance" or something like that. He had the most beautiful voice and had a natural talent as a singer which was never fully appreciated.' Joy sang a few bars of the song to demonstrate the interpretation he would give the ending when really on form, and to emphasize the tenderness and sensitivity he could bring to his singing.

The Bevs also remembered the marvellous carriage of the man — 'He had a beautiful walk,' said Teddie — and how different he was from his cocky, swanky image. They said he didn't mix much but always had a queue of dukes, duchesses, earls and other nobility knocking at his dressing-room door at the Palladium. Joy said that, when they got to know him better, they would invite him down to their room and he would enjoy a cup of tea with them.

At one time the Beverley Sisters had a letter of introduction from Cecil Madden of the BBC to Bing Crosby, which they used, and Bing said he had heard a lot about them. When they explained that they had worked a lot with Bob and he always used them, Bing said how lucky they were, adding; 'It was the luckiest day of my life when I teamed up with him.' Then, the girls recalled, he laughed and said: 'But don't you ever tell him I said so!' Babs said: 'We never did tell him, but now all this time later and with poor old Bing no longer with us, we're happy to be quoted on it, and if Bob gets to know, we haven't told him!'

The girls said: 'For all his greatness, Bob hasn't lost his humility, yet nobody tells Bob Hope what to do.' When I asked them about his writers and reliance on cue cards, they were in total agreement and very positive: 'The big joke about Bob was the one about when he got down to nine writers he was ad-libbing. But he was a great ad-libber. He was the first comedian to use the topical gag so extensively, and he needed so much material that it was sensible to rely on gag-writers. It was the only thing to do. But don't let anyone kid you that he couldn't operate except by reading cards. Even when he hadn't got his cards, he was razor sharp.'

The Beverley Sisters were remembering a period when the London Palladium specialized in bringing the great American entertainers to Britain. In August alone the following year, 1953, they headlined Bud Abbott and Lou Costello, Frankie Laine and the sensational recording celebrity Kay Starr, and on 14 September Bob Hope was back by popular demand for a further two-week engagement.

While it is true that Bob's gigantic reputation and popularity with the British public had been built on radio shows and films which compromised little on the American sense of humour — and his non-American fans seemed able to accept his material in that form, it was different when he was standing on a British stage performing live to a British audience. The good-natured 'slandering' of popular figures which in America had to be about Americans, in Britain had to be about people in public life to whom British audiences could specifically relate. Of course, some celebrities were universal. His cracks about Bing Crosby, Jack Benny, George Burns, Frank Sinatra, Fred Astaire and Ginger Rogers, Danny Kaye and others always received an immediate response, but to help him infuse some 'British' material into his act he engaged for a number of years the talented British scriptwriting team of Denis Goodwin and Bob Monkhouse.

Bob Monkhouse, still popular on British television as one of the smoothest, funniest comedians with a lasting reputation, remembers his Bob Hope writing days vividly. He told me: 'Both Denis and I revered him. He was very demanding to work for, a slave-driver, and you certainly earned your money when you worked for Hope. He was a prodigious worker and expected everybody to be the same. I remember once at the Dorchester

Hotel, we had been working for him through a long, wearying session and I went out to the lavatory. Bob reminded me that while I was there, as I obviously had plenty of paper in with me, there was no need to stop working.

'Another time, at the Savoy, he caught me taking a quick break and asked what I thought I was doing, having a paid vacation? He was great for that sort of thing. He would get his message across in the form of a gag, but often there would be a serious sting there that he made sure you couldn't fail to notice.'

Bob said their relationship started casually enough while Bob Hope was working in Britain. 'Denis and I had been writing successfully for artists like Jerry Desmonde and Jack Buchanan and were keen for Bob Hope to notice our work. He was a star of enormous stature and we were in awe of him and couldn't possibly have made any kind of personal approach to him direct. That would have been out of the question. So we asked Jerry and Jack if they could help, and they mentioned us to him and let him see some of our material.'

Bob Monkhouse says they first wrote for Hope in 1953. 'But he had been my hero since I was a small boy. I saw him first in 1939 through his films and now have many of his early pictures in my private library at home, including *Going Spanish*, which he made for Educational way back in 1934, the very first film he ever made.

Bob and Denis became Bob Hope's regular writers whenever he came to Britain, and in 1959 Denis went to America to join the Bob Hope writing team. Monkhouse didn't go with him because by then his own career as a performer had advanced and in addition he had a young family whom he wanted to stay close to. Said Bob Monkhouse: 'Bob Hope was enormously kind to Denis, who was shy and was given a hard time by quite a number of Hope's regular American writers, perhaps with the exception of Charlie Lee who, along with Bob, kept a benevolent eye on Denis and looked after him at a difficult time.'

Denis Goodwin returned to Britain and, sadly, died in 1975, still only in his mid-forties.

Bob said Hope was a daunting figure, with a laser beam in his glance, and had enormous presence. Despite being a comedian and constantly poking fun at himself, he had a great kind of sexual charge and was a popular character, particularly with women.

But Hope had some strange characteristics, observed Bob

Monkhouse. 'We worked for him for a number of years and produced tens of thousands of jokes, but it was very hard to get him to pay up. We nearly always had to ask for it. We never received a cheque in all the time we worked for him. It was always a money order or dollars — and he always wanted a receipt,' said Bob.

Monkhouse said Hope was brilliant at assessing gags. 'I've never seen him make a mistake. He would make up his mind quickly, sorting out the main jokes and assembling on one side what are known as the page-fillers. Sometimes, against his better judgement, he would include a gag or two which had been recommended to him and, although he gave all material the same treatment and put all his gags over with that impressive style, timing and delivery, invariably those which he had been doubtful about didn't go down well. He never seemed to be wrong.'

Bob said he and Denis got to know the way Hope worked when given a batch of gags to go through. 'After a while we noticed that he tended to skip through the early material and also that his concentration would be flagging before he got to the end. So we began to put our best jokes in the middle of the material, when his concentration was at its highest.'

Bob Monkhouse agrees with the Beverley Sisters about Hope's ability to ad-lib. 'His own joke rebounded on him,' he said. 'He needed his writers simply because of the enormous volume of topical material he used, but when he saw the media reaction to them he joked it up. It was the same with the idiot cards. He needed them, of course, but he deliberately used them as gags which were put over with such conviction that many people believed he couldn't ad-lib. But this is totally wrong. He has an extraordinary ability to ad-lib.' Bob Monkhouse recalled an astonishing example of his talent at a Palladium daytime show in the mid-1950s: 'He worked an hour and a half non-stop with no script and with the audience firing questions at him, and he ad-libbed totally throughout the whole proceedings. It was an amazing demonstration.'

He reckons Bob Hope established his 'persona' years ago, for when he was interviewing him as recently as 1982 Hope was the same as he had been on film years before. 'Though he so typifies the basic American style of humour, he has a unique quality and stature,' said Bob. 'A truly great performer.'

Bob Hope was back at the Palladium in November 1954 for a

Royal Variety Performance in front of Her Majesty The Queen. He was the headliner, assisted by Moira Lister and Jerry Desmonde, with 'The Hope Repertory Company'. Many British stars at the top of their profession were also on the bill, including trumpeter Eddie Calvert, Richard Hearne ('Mr Pastry'), Arthur Askey, Max Bygraves, Flanagan and Allen, Al Reed, Norman Wisdom, David Whitfield, Dickie Valentine, Ted Heath, Jack Parnell, Noel Coward and Shirley Eaton. American stars supporting Hope included Frankie Laine and Howard Keel. Little wonder that Bob regarded the Palladium as the greatest vaudeville theatre in the world!

Shirley Eaton had been acting since she was twelve, and though she made nearly thirty films and was popular on television, she did not reach the peak of her fame until she was 'painted to death' in the James Bond movie *Goldfinger* in 1964 — she abandoned acting in 1968. She was only seventeen when she appeared on the same bill as Bob Hope in front of Her Majesty and looks back on that brief encounter as a rather special interlude in her life. Shirley was in France when we talked on the phone, and she remembered those days thirty-four years ago.

'He was very sweet to me. Although I had been doing quite a bit of television work, I was surprised to be chosen to do a short sketch with him at the Royal Variety Show at the Palladium. I don't remember how it came about that I was chosen. I was young and he was such a big star, but he was charming and quite adorable.'

Shirley also remembers Bob Hope when she appeared with him in a Hollywood film more than ten years later. She told me: 'I had just finished filming *The Scorpio Letters* for MGM over in Hollywood and was in the studio restaurant one day when Bob Hope walked in. I was due to return to Britain in a week or two. He saw me at the table and remembered me. He came over and we chatted for a while. He was very nice, asked me what I had been doing, and before we had finished talking he asked me if I would like to appear opposite him in a film he was about to do. I hedged a bit and told him I was just about to return home, but he was persuasive and I ended up staying in Hollywood for another six or seven weeks filming with him.'

The film they did together was the United Artists picture *Eight on the Lam* (*Eight on the Run,* in Britain).

'He was great, a nice and friendly man to work with,' said

Shirley. 'Of course, he liked his own way, but he didn't upstage you, no more than would be reasonable to expect from any comedian with his kind of enthusiasm, and he always did it with such a twinkle in his eye that you couldn't possibly be hurt by it. Like most top American artists, he tended to have his entourage around him, but once you were taken into the circle, he was lovely, not overbearing and always very professional.'

Shirley, who has had a home in France for fifteen years, said she has regular reminders of the happy times she spent working with Hope. 'I still get a Christmas card from him, every year,' she said with obvious pleasure.

In the mid-1950s, by then over fifty years old, Bob was virtually doing the commuter run to Britain, for he was back again in 1956 at the request of the great Sir Lawrence Olivier, to appear at the Palladium once more in a star-studded charity presentation called *Night of 100 Stars*. That glittering occasion began at midnight, and Bob was still on stage at 3 a.m. cracking jokes about Crosby and Jack Benny, despite his scheduled return flight to America just five hours later.

To his delight, the 1960s continued to bring him frequently to the UK. In 1961 he was over for the charity première of *Bachelor in Paradise,* the movie he made for MGM with Lana Turner and Janis Paige. On the return flight, it is claimed that, totally coincidentally, the selected film was *Bachelor in Paradise!* Bob said that it was the first time he had seen one of his pictures on an airplane. 'At least nobody walked out,' he quipped.

He was soon back, this time for a much longer stay. Two of his writers, Norman Panama and Mel Frank, had come up with the idea of doing another *Road* film — there hadn't been one for some ten years. Made by United Artists, it was decided to shoot *Road to Hong Kong* in Britain, at Shepperton Studios. Since it would be a three-month stay, Bob and Bing brought their families with them. They thought originally they would stay in London, but then Mel Frank, encouraged by Dolores, searched for somewhere they could rent and came up with Cranbourne Court, a large country mansion near Windsor with twenty-five acres of grounds and twenty-two bedrooms, fully equipped with china, silver and full staff, including an Arthur Treacher-like butler. It was big enough for the two families to move into together, with space to spare, but even more appetizing for Bob and Bing was that both the Sunningdale and Wentworth golf courses were close at hand!

Bob remembered the visit: 'In the morning Bing and I sailed off to the studio, only fourteen minutes away, in our chauffeured Rolls-Royce. Our wives and kiddies explored merry olde England while we toiled away under the arc lamps. Well, it wasn't too terribly strenuous. When the English crew broke for tea in the afternoon, Bing and I took a golf break. We could usually get in nine holes before darkness fell over the bogs.'

Two other incidents which Bob Hope describes in his autobiography *Where There's Life* concern his fanaticism for golf. He and Bing were in the habit of dashing off as soon as there was a sufficient break in shooting. On one occasion he had been doing a harem scene when he was required to have his toe-nails painted. He rushed off to Wentworth and afterwards was discussing his game with what he described as a couple of Colonel Blimp types. 'I pulled off my spiked shoes and golf socks and gazed down in horror at my toe-nails, which looked like an Iceland sunset,' he recalled. 'The two club members saw the same sight and stared with open mouths. I tried to act debonair. It was one of my best performances!'

Another time he and Bing rushed immediately from the set after a scene in which they had been given a hero's welcome. He went to the locker room for a shower and nodded to a couple of dour gentlemen who were about to retire to the clubroom for their gin and bitters. Said Bob: 'As I peeled off my jockey shorts, a handful of confetti fell out.'

Bob and Dolores look back with fond memories to the time they spent at Cranbourne Court while making *Road to Hong Kong,* even though it was to turn out to be the final film in the fabulously successful series.

In November 1967 he was back again at the London Palladium, performing once more for Her Majesty The Queen in another Royal Variety Performance. This time he topped a bill which included Lulu, Sandie Shaw, Dickie Henderson, Rolf Harris, Val Doonican, Tommy Cooper, Harry Secombe, Ken Dodd, Vicki Carr and the then new singing sensation, Tom Jones.

Bob simply couldn't keep away from Britain, and frequently now doing charity performances. As early as 1951 he had donated to a Camberwell boys' club his entire earnings from a show at London's Prince of Wales Theatre — £15,000. The money was used to convert an old bomb-site into a haven for youngsters, and he continued to support the venture for a number of years.

The number of personal appearances he was prepared to make for charity became legendary and in 1970, approaching sixty-seven years of age, he followed up a gruelling 100,000-mile tour of the United States with two performances at the Royal Festival Hall in front of Princess Alexandra and then one for Princess Anne and Prince Charles, as part of a glittering *Night of Nights* charity concert in which he shared top billing with Frank Sinatra in aid of United World Colleges.

This was one of many charities actively supported by Lord Mountbatten, who had arranged for Sir Noel Coward to be compère. Only twenty-four hours before the show was to open, the seventy-year-old playwright was rushed to St Thomas's Hospital in London suffering from pleurisy. Jeffrey Archer, who at that time was the charity's public relations officer recruited to organize gala evenings, appealed to Mountbatten for help in finding a suitable replacement.

A number of names were raised, but Archer, shrewdly tactical, suggested that what was really needed was a major celebrity, someone who could be tempted to appear only through the enormous influence of Mountbatten. 'Grace Kelly,' said Archer. Mountbatten dismissed the idea as being impossible, for only a few weeks before Prince Rainier had said that his wife would never go on the stage again. But Mountbatten was persuaded to try, and somehow he managed to win them both over. Princess Grace stepped in for Sir Noel Coward in a blaze of publicity and with her help, along with Sinatra, Hope and others, that one evening raised half a million pounds for the charity.

Then came Bob's 'surprise' appearance in a special two-part edition of *This is Your Life*. Thames Television had been planning the show for about a year and, with the staff of the Savoy Hotel sworn to secrecy, had booked his four children into the hotel where Bob was also staying with Dolores. He had no idea they were there. He had known of the impending 'surprise' for some weeks, but when Eamonn Andrews voiced one of the most famous phrases on television, he looked impressively surprised. 'Come on,' he drawled. 'You're kidding.' It was a standard Bob Hope phrase.

A whole army of his British relatives enjoyed their moment in the limelight. Earl Mountbatten was there, along with Tony Bennett and an old girlfriend of Bob's from forty years before, and in a television interview screened from America President Nixon said his country was particularly indebted to Britain for giving them Bob Hope, not only for his qualities as an entertainer but also as a man. 'I am proud to know him as a friend,' he declared. Shirley Eaton told me from France that it was a disappointment for her not to be there. 'I was ill at the time,' she said.

A few days later Bob was again giving his services free in a star cabaret at the *Talk of the Town* in London which was to raise more than £100,000 for the World Wildlife Fund. Billed along with him were Engelbert Humperdinck, Petula Clark and Glenn Campbell, with Rex Harrison as the compère. The Queen, Prince Philip, as chairman of the fund, and other members of the royal family were in the audience, as well as royalty from the Netherlands, Spain, Denmark, Luxembourg and Belgium. By now Bob was on such firm ground with the royal family that his well-targeted yet proprietorial one-liners delivered with such precision and timing from the stage were enjoyed as much by those who were the subject of the jokes as by the public. One wisecrack blended effortlessly into the next as his smooth, immaculate performance gathered pace and pitch: '. . . and I've never seen such royalty. I really never have. This whole thing looks like a chess game — live . . .'

Two days later he was on the stage of the Albert Hall as the featured star guest during the televised 1970 Miss World contest. In December that year, with the new Miss World and sultry actress Ursula Andress, he was entertaining American servicemen at the Lakenheath, Suffolk, base at the start of his twentieth Christmas tour.

More than 5,000 Americans packed into a hangar to laugh, cheer and applaud as for two hours Bob joked and sang, bringing in numerous good-natured digs at Britain from an American's point of view. The weather, of course: 'Most servicemen are decorated with ribbons. Here it's mildew.' And, 'You're the only servicemen I know who top your commendation ribbons with a cluster of mushrooms.' His legendary cue cards were well in evidence — fifty pounds of them at Lakenheath. Altogether they were reckoned to weigh something like two tons for just one round-the-world Christmas show for the US armed forces.

The overall success of Bob's British appearances in 1970 was marred by two incidents — a surprising below-par performance at the Festival Hall charity presentation, and 'feminist' demonstrators who somehow infiltrated the televising of the Miss World finals and caused Bob to walk off stage in disgust. They disrupted the event with flour bags, stink bombs, paint and ink, missiles and placards, fireworks, shouts and screams to such an extent that in the chaos that followed there was little he could do but walk away.

The Beverley Sisters agree that Bob was very annoyed and bitterly disappointed about the demonstration, when he had flour bags and other missiles pitched his way, but really they said they wished he could have seen it as a compliment, for that is what it was. Babs said she personally knew some of the demonstrators and they picked what they considered would be the greatest moment on television to raise public consciousness for their cause — women's lib. 'We were sorry for Bob when they did it because he was terribly upset, but it had nothing to do with him personally.'

He had the sympathy of most of the British public, but not altogether of the British Press, some papers condemning him for what they considered his faint-hearted action. Some commentators were convinced that he was both angered and upset by what he considered totally unjust criticism of his action at the Miss World contest. For a time it seems likely that the incident sullied his love-affair with Britain. Whatever the reason, the fact is that he didn't appear professionally in Britain for another seven years.

Despite Bob's 'fun' image and easy, relaxed style as a professional entertainer, he always harboured firm views on the issues which he felt to be particularly important, especially where they affected him personally, and was not deflected by controversy. Perhaps his early reluctance to follow the trend and try his hand in Hollywood was the first innocent reflection of this element of his character.

Another trait which developed with his growing fame was his protection of the innermost elements of his family life. In interviews he would talk freely about his wife, children, associates and friends, his homes, his background, even the money he was making, though he steadfastly hedged when it came to how much he was worth in total — perhaps he didn't know, genuinely. He would do interviews in the grounds of his home, but always barred photographs being taken inside any of his houses. Even his dear relatives from Britain had to observe that particular rule.

At the peak of his Hollywood career, as we have noted, he made a stand against the dictatorial attitude of the studios, whose policy was to pay their stars for the work they did, while the studio collected all the profits themselves. Their argument was that they were in the risk business and they stood the loss if a picture was a failure, while the star's money was guaranteed. But in the boom days of Hollywood the risks were slender, and the take from worldwide distribution could be phenomenal. In 1946, for example, Paramount made a profit of $39 million against $13 million in 1942. At the valuations of forty-two years ago, this kind of business performance by even the best of American standards was considered gigantic.

Bob Hope decided it was fundamentally wrong that the stars of the films which made such money for the studios (for it was the stars who brought the public to the box office) should not be allowed a stake in the profits. He wanted the opportunity to make pictures in conjunction with Paramount but through a film company of his own which he proposed to set up. Paramount rejected the idea totally and for a year Bob didn't make a movie. But he was simply too big an attraction to be ignored and a reconciliation was eventually struck which gave him what he wanted.

Despite his gigantic reputation he kept in touch with his relatives in Britain.

In 1980, when Bob's cousin Frank Symons and his wife Kathleen celebrated their golden wedding in Hitchin, Bob and Dolores didn't send them a present. A year later, Dolores assured them: 'We haven't forgotten your golden wedding.' What Bob and his wife had been cooking up was revealed to Frank and Kathleen in 1982, when they received a surprise telegram: 'Can you come for a holiday on 5 April? Tickets are waiting for you at Heathrow.' For what turned out to be a magnificent golden wedding anniversary present and the holiday of a lifetime, Frank and Kathleen spent five weeks in the United States as the guests of Bob and Dolores, including two weeks at the Hopes' Palm Springs home. The rest of the time was spent enjoying the luxury of American hotels throughout the country.

Said Frank: 'Everything was arranged for us by Bob and

Dolores. They went out of their way to make us feel at home and they introduced us to a lot of famous people, including Mary Martin, the mother of ''JR'', former president Gerald Ford and his wife, and the old movie actress, Janet Gaynor.'

But this was more than a visit for Frank, Kathleen and their daughter Jean Nixon simply to see the sights. Thoughtfully, Bob and Dolores had arranged for them to visit Cleveland, where Bob's father, Frank's uncle, had worked as a stonemason when first landing in America more than seventy years before. For Bob and Dolores there were moments of intense nostalgia. There was a tour of the old Palace Theatre, where Bob had played to record crowds with his famous sidekicks of the day, Frances Langford and Jerry Colonna. He remembered how his brother Ivor's eyes had bulged when he saw Bob pick up a cheque for $20,000 in the 1940s, when he filled the 3,400-seater Palace to the rafters.

The party also visited Cleveland's Presbyterian church in Euclid Avenue. Looking up at the Gothic architecture, Bob said quietly: 'This is the church my father helped build.' At another point of the tour, Bob, just twenty-three days away from his seventy-ninth birthday and perhaps mindful of his own mortality, looked up. 'It's a masterpiece,' he said. 'This will be around a long time after I'm gone.'

By this time Bob had become a firm target for anti-Vietnam protestors, but to Frank and Kathleen Symons he was not only a famous Hollywood film star they could swank about back home but a true and enduring friend who genuinely valued the company and companionship of his old relatives.

6 A Long, Long Trail

Bob's radio status had developed over the years until, by the time radio was at the height of its power and influence as a means of mass communication and entertainment, he was well entrenched as one of its top performers. To many vaudevillians the upstart medium of radio was despised, but others, with the vision or opportunity to become part of it during its years of enormous development in the 1930s, became famous with a speed impossible for the touring stage performer. Jack Benny, Burns and Allen and Al Jolson were already radio stars by the time Bob made his early broadcasts, making life hard for those still to make their mark. His first tentative openings were in the Sunday morning *Capitol Family Hour* put out from New York's Capitol Theatre, and in the *Fleischman Hour* with Rudy Vallee as the star. Bob was unfamiliar with the technique of working in radio, with no audience to work to, and uneasy because of it. He had been in the business too long to contemplate overnight success and continued sensibly with his stage career, mixing in the occasional radio appearance, as he got the chance, in shows like the *RKO Theatre of the Air* before gaining a featured spot in the *Bromo Seltzer Intimate Hour* in 1935.

Unlike in the UK, radio in the United States was sponsored, and companies labelled their shows with their name, or the name of one of their products. Because of this commercial approach, listening figures were a vital yardstick, and as the *Bromo Seltzer* show fell away in the ratings, and was then withdrawn, Bob returned to the theatre circuit with Dolores. A couple of brief radio appearances led to a significant breakthrough when, in mid-1937, he signed a twenty-six-week contract for the *Woodbury Soap Show*. This continued to run once he had moved to Hollywood for *The Big Broadcast of 1938,* special arrangements being made, as mentioned earlier, for him to continue with the show through a transcontinental hook-up.

Bob Hope's need for a live audience to feed from and react to took on critical proportions during that first broadcast from Hollywood. He had assumed there would be a studio audience and was devastated when he realized there wasn't going to be one. What followed has long since passed into the folklore of Hope.

With the co-operation of ventriloquist Edgar Bergen, who was broadcasting from an adjacent studio, he managed to persuade an usher to let him divert the audience leaving the Bergen broadcast into his own broadcast studio, where, no doubt to their astonishment, they found themselves the audience for Bob Hope's show.

At around this time Bob advanced his radio reputation with guest spots and then as a regular performer on the Lucky Strike sponsored *Your Hollywood Parade,* headed by singer-actor Dick Powell, already a major Hollywood star. The programme ran for an hour and included a pleasant mixture of music, singing, comedy, news and gossip about Hollywood and the stars, interviews, reviews and so on. Rosemary Lane, one of the three Lane sisters who made such an impact in Hollywood in 1938 with such box-office successes as *Four Daughters* and *Four Wives,* was a regular singer on the programme, and the famous Al Goodman Orchestra was also featured. Despite much promise the show ran for only a short time, but long enough for Bob Hope to make an important impact with his five-minute monologue slots.

Breaking new ground for radio with a repertoire of highly topical gags, his reputation soared. The topicality, the relaxed delivery and the impeccable, seemingly effortless timing gave no hint of the tedious and painstaking preparation he would go through to have things right. Dolores revealed years later: 'He would work for hours to get those few minutes exactly as he wanted them.' Bob's rapid, if relaxed, delivery would devour scores of one- and two-liners during the course of just one five-minute spot, and his insistence on topicality added further pressures as transmission time approached. With such topical material it was too much for one person, even Bob Hope, to be the provider and the front man, and it was at about this time that he began his policy of hiring writers.

He had no cause to be depressed by the cancellation of *Your Hollywood Parade.* Senior executives of the advertising agency involved in putting on the show had been so impressed with his work that they were well into negotiations with his radio agent, Jimmy Saphier, by the time the programme came off the air. They wanted Bob to front his own show for a major sponsored programme then in preparation.

The only hitch to the signing of this important deal was Bob himself. The streak of stubborn independence, with which he was later to confront the production chiefs at Paramount in a similar situation, was at this point used to achieve his own aims on radio. In cash terms he quickly got what he wanted — a reputed $3,000 per show to start and building to $5,000 per show during the course of his six-year contract. For 1938–44 these fees were impressive, but he also insisted on having substantial control of creative and production issues. This unusual and, as seen by many close associates, unreasonable condition was to prove significant and pertinent to the ultimate success of the shows. It is doubtful if the highly personal approach which Bob developed in the shows which emerged would have seen the light of day had he not been able to run things very much his own way.

This was the series sponsored by *Pepsodent*. The first transmission was in September 1938 and over the years it was to project Bob Hope to the very top of the radio ratings. His retinue of accredited artists became part of the Hope establishment on the *Pepsodent Show*, known to an enormous public. Jerry Colonna is the best remembered, but there were also announcer Bill Goodwin, bandleader Skinnay Ennis and the remarkably talented musical group, Six Hits and a Miss. Bob's programme for Pepsodent made stars of them all. He devised his own particular format, leaning heavily on a small army of talented writers to provide the sketch and monologue material required for each show. He was hard on his writers. They each had to submit a script for each show and, although the final transmission would be half an hour in length, they had to write enough for sixty or ninety minutes. At the gruelling script conference and pruning procedures which followed, there was no room for sympathy, understanding, benevolence, compassion, solace, mitigation or consolation. The best jokes stayed in, the remainder came out.

During rehearsals — and indeed during all stages leading up to the time the show went on the air — even good material would be unceremoniously axed to slash the running time or because Bob thought it better without it. The show would then be presented before a live audience and recorded. Even during this 'dummy run' Bob would scrap jokes instantly if they didn't get a good response. Next day, as he ran the recording, there would be further cutting and changes to gain extra pace, polish, impact and appeal, and to give a final trimming to ensure there was no risk of over-running. It was a punitive, tortuous routine, but it assured that Bob would have only the very best material for his show. That point was proved by the acclaim of the vast American public, and the remarkable response of the professional critics. In the country's 'Best Comedian' category, Bob Hope went into fourth place, and the very next year, 1940, they voted him first ahead of Jack Benny.

The main radio competition for Bob Hope in those days came from Jack Benny and Fred Allen. They were older and had been headliners for some time before Bob began to challenge their positions. While his style owed something to both, it was in a sense highly individual. He was brasher, perhaps more super-ficial, certainly more adventurous and courageous in the material he used. Because of his ridicule and castigation of public figures, along with himself and other members of the team, the Pepsodent top brass nursed some misgivings over his choice of material before finally giving in to his demands for virtual control of his programmes. They considered he could occasionally sail too close to the wind with gags which carried sexual innuendo, and warned him about it. In making a judgement on this, however, one must remember the influence and importance of the sponsor in American radio programmes and their almost paranoic determination not to cause offence to anyone, in case it turned them away from their products. By today's standards Hope's material was, and indeed still is on his rare public appearances, as innocent as Snow White and in any event would always carry that disarming quality calculated to make any dubious gag inoffensive.

The shows were a mixture of sketches, pairings with guest artists, musical numbers and, most important, Hope's mono-logues and were continued successfully for more than a decade as part of America's staple diet, in peace and war, and then again in peace.

Bob had become an extraordinary entertainer, excelling in films and on radio, and in huge demand for personal appear-ances. He was an international institution. His schedule

Top billing for Bob at the London Palladium, the most famous variety theatre in the world. Sharing the bill were the Beverley Sisters who remember Bob with affection.

Life-long friends – Bob and Bing out for some useful practice at the Temple Golf Course, Maidenhead, in September 1952.

Bob and Dolores' adopted children, Linda and Tony (back) and Kelly and Nora. They grew up knowing they were adopted.

The impressive Hope homestead in North Hollywood, always considered the 'family home' according to Linda Hope.

One more Road to travel and who can resist the beckoning
invitation of Dorothy Lamour? *Road to Bali* was the sixth
in the series.

Jane Russell 'materializes' in *Road to Bali* in 1952. The film also
featured Humphrey Bogart and Katherine Hepburn pulling
'The African Queen'.

A dramatic example of Hope's generosity was the help he gave to London's Clubland for youngsters in 1951. With Revd Jimmy Butterworth and Vivien Hill he visited the restored premises.

Meeting the Queen after the Royal Variety Show at the London Palladium in 1956. Also in the line-up are Frankie Laine, Norman Wisdom and David Whitfield.

Shrove Tuesday fun with Diana Dors in 1956 at Pinewood Studios.

Proud pop with Linda
(nineteen) and Tony
(eighteen) arriving
in London from St Louis
in 1958.

Looking like a craft from
outer space, the Hope's
new home in Palm
'Springs took nine years
to complete and cost
three million dollars
to build.

Back together again after a lapse of nearly ten years – Bob, Bing and Dotty hit the final *Road to Hong Kong* (1961), twenty-one years after making the first film in the series.

Bob approaching fifty and one of the biggest radio and movie stars
in the world.

included army camp shows in America, overseas tours entertaining troops (which took in the south-west Pacific, when he
travelled some 30,000 miles and gave around 150 shows), radio
commitments for Pepsodent (for whom he would sign a new ten-
year contract at a reputed one million dollars a year), special
shows for President Roosevelt and, in time, President Truman,
and a new career as a highly successful author.

Bob's troop entertaining during the Second World War had
given him a privileged insight into the way GIs lived miles from
home in army camps and on overseas bases. He had
accumulated dozens of hastily scribbled notes of names,
incidents and snatches of conversation, and recalled the stories
behind his souvenirs and memorabilia. This material, together
with the vast store of personal anecdotes which was still vivid in
his mind, was assembled to form a unique documentation which
was to become a bestselling book.

With the help of writers he was already contributing regular
columns to newspapers and a magazine or two, but this was a
much more ambitious project. A writer friend, Carroll Carroll,
worked on the manuscript, and the book finally emerged as a
fascinating, amusing, absorbing and compassionate account
under the inspiring title of *I Never Left Home.* The title was Bob's
idea and alluded to the fact that he kept coming across many
people he knew during his wartime troop entertaining. The
100,000 copies of the softback one-dollar version were quickly
supplemented by another 100,000 print run in hardback, and in
little more than a year well over 1 ½ million copies were sold. He
later turned author again and, with Carroll's help, put together
all the bits and pieces from his South Pacific and European USO
tours. The result was *So This Is Peace,* generally not considered as
good as the earlier title but nonetheless again a bestseller with
million plus sales.

Nothing lasts forever and in 1948 Bob found it necessary to
make changes to his radio programme in the face of the mounting wrath of critics who found the same old format, the same old
people, had become stale. So far the listening public had not
shown any major swing away from him, but he feared they
might if the criticism was ignored. Unsure, he brought in
featured female singers and courageously dropped his old friend
Jerry Colonna, along with another regular, Barbara Jo Allen.

By 1949, with the show now sponsored by Lever Brothers,

radio was increasingly under threat from television. As it engulfed the nation in the next few years, radio struggled to find a new role. Ultimately it would have no place for the format which had dominated the 1930s and '40s.

Bob Hope was a power force in radio entertainment when radio was the all-powerful medium, but the end was in sight. He would become an even bigger draw on television than he had been on radio, but for the time being, with his personal ratings falling, one can imagine how it must have satisfied his professional vanity and his particularly sharp sense of business to be offered a $2 million contract to switch to daytime radio, appearing after breakfast in a Monday-to-Friday show sponsored by General Foods, and in a weekly variety show put out in the evening. It gave his flagging radio career a new lease of life. The fee for the first season was the biggest ever paid in the history of radio, but General Foods obviously considered it good value for money. They stayed with Hope for five successful years, until 1958 when he felt the time was right for him to move on — to television.

Bob Hope has shown outstanding professional durability. He personifies the legend of entertainment super-stardom and even well into the 1980s the mere hint that he will appear for a moment or two as a guest on *This is Your Life* or be present at a special occasion is enough to quicken the pulse and cause a ripple of excitement. Advancing years seem unable to deplete him. The relaxed manner, the sharp eyes, the even sharper wit, the topical gag and, perhaps above all, the perfection of the art of timing, continue to single him out as the supreme master of his art.

It was surely, however, in the 1940s and '50s that Bob Hope's career in all its facets was at its peak. He made his best films then. He dominated radio. His programme of personal appearances in America, Britain, France and elsewhere, both for money and for charity, was at its most energetic. He moved successfully into television, carving out an even bigger career in the new medium than he had enjoyed on radio, and was the natural first choice as compère at all the most glittering gala occasions including, of course, the Oscar presentation ceremonies. It was also at this period that he began a separate career entertaining the American forces, especially those stationed overseas.

It began simply enough in 1941 when he went to the Army Air

Force base at March Field, Riverside in California, not a hundred miles from home. It would be nice to think that it was his idea and that it emerged from a sense of duty or dedication to the national cause, but that didn't come until later, after the US had entered the war.

Credit for the March Field experiment goes to Bob's Pepsodent show producer, Al Capstaff, who put the idea to Bob one day after rehearsal. Bob's instant reaction was cool, but during the conversation his interest grew and as they parted he asked Capstaff to work out more details so that they could talk about it again.

As a professional entertainer Bob could see the potential in taking the show live to some 2,000 servicemen. It was a new idea, bound to capture attention. The decision made, the results more than justified the inconvenience and established a pattern which was to gain him a highly respected reputation as troop entertainer *par excellence* over more years than he now cares to remember.

Two similar shows took place within the next three weeks, the first at the San Diego Naval Station when Bob had film celebrity Priscilla Lane as his featured guest, and then at the Marine base of San Luis, Obispo. At his next show, from the Army base of Camp Callan, Mary Martin was his guest. The pattern had now been set, and after the Japanese bombed Pearl Harbor, his camp shows took on a greater, more significant meaning.

For a short time Bob toured only domestic locations, but once America had entered the war it wasn't long before he and his team headed out to the main areas of troop concentration.

The idea of using the shows he gave for the forces for his radio programmes was a great success, and more than 400 were broadcast during the 1940s. In addition he made countless other appearances, sometimes giving three and four performances in a day, in a whirlwind programme which was phenomenal in its intensity and for its physical and mental demands. He also took part in a variety of other troop shows broadcast in both America and Europe.

Bob's style of comedy suited the armed forces perfectly. He became one of the boys, a buddy and a friend. The uniformed audiences loved him when he launched into his quick-fire gags about Crosby, Jack Benny and other 'established' targets, and whistled themselves hoarse when he talked knowingly about the curvaceous Dorothy Lamour, Jane Russell and the other 'glamour girls' who had starred with him in his Hollywood pictures.

They loved him most of all when he took the side of the ordinary soldier, sailor or airman against the 'privileged' officer ranks. The tactic was not new. British comedians had made themselves popular with similar pointed jokes before America came into the war. But Bob did it earlier perhaps, and certainly with more success, than any other troop entertainer in America. There were no sacred areas. He poked fun at politicians, officers, the enemy, other entertainers, service life with its restrictions, rations and uniforms, and he gagged about girl-friends, wives and home leave. Most of all he made fun of himself, his own life, family, golfing, co-stars and visits to different places.

The jokes came thick and fast, whether planned or impromptu. The fluency and timing were impeccable. Because he concentrated so much on topicality, many of his gags from that time, which were focused so sharply on the overriding issues of the day, do not stand up well to repetition now. But at the time, nine out of ten hit the jackpot, striking some kind of chord with servicemen many miles from home.

At one show he talked about the plane he had arrived in. He said it was very small, so small in fact that at one point he asked the pilot if he didn't think he should gain more altitude. 'What for?' asked the pilot. 'It's cooler here under the trees.' Before leaving for home, he told troops in Alaska: 'Be happy, you guys. Be proud! You know what you are — you're God's frozen people.'

As the schedule of Bob's service shows increased, the tempo of his life built up to a frightening pace. His troop entertaining alone would have provided sufficient stimulus for many entertainers, but he somehow managed to squeeze this into a life which included radio shows from the studio, personal appear-ances, picture-making in Hollywood, interviews, home life with Dolores and their children, meetings with agents, producers and advisers, and inevitably rounds of golf as often as he could manage.

He wasn't put off when carefully worked-out plans had to be changed. The trip he made to Alaska with Jerry Colonna, singer Frances Langford and guitarist Tony Romano probably wouldn't have happened had he not persisted. When they first began to work out the plans, it seemed impossible that they could fly to Alaska, entertain the troops and be back in time to do the scheduled Pepsodent radio show from the studio. Bob was just completing one of the two films he did with Sam Goldwyn and was already cutting things fine by suggesting that, if shooting finished on Saturday 5 September, they could fly to Alaska on Tuesday, spend ten days there, get back to Seattle for the radio show, then set off to do more entertaining for troops in Washington and Oregon states, before returning to Seattle for their second radio show on 29 September.

When the base at Alaska couldn't guarantee that weather conditions would enable the schedule to go through as planned, and said there was always the risk of their not getting back in time for the radio show, the trip seemed doomed. But Bob persisted, cabling the military authorities in Alaska to tell them he would take responsibility and was prepared to take the risk of not getting back to do the radio show.

The tour proved enormously successful. The troupe gave shows everywhere and anywhere: on the backs of trucks, in small huts, in larger halls. The entertaining was virtually non-stop from early morning to late evening. Bad weather gave them a rough flight from one base to another and almost prevented their making the first radio show back in Seattle, but they did make it . . . just. Then, instead of taking the easy trip around Washington and Oregon as he contemplated, they returned to the wilds of Alaska on Bob's say-so, and spent another five days with the troops up there. After that it was back to Seattle for the second radio show and then on to Hollywood, where Bob asked Paramount to delay his next movie, *Let's Face It,* so he could fit in more troop shows.

Bob wasn't in uniform during the war, but no serviceman or woman could have given more commitment to the war effort. His schedule was unflagging and the pressure was so intense that Dolores feared he might crack under the strain of continually travelling from one location to another, crowding in unscheduled shows to bring joy and pleasure to sometimes just a handful of men.

His endless round of hospital visits lifted the spirits of the wounded. There was no sloppy sentimentality. He was supreme at assessing the atmosphere in a ward or the tensions in a forward first-aid post. Appropriately, he was sympathetic and understanding but at other times he challenged patients to face up to their problems and even joked about their injuries. Two of the best examples of his wartime morale-boosting style have been used before, in the book *The Amazing Careers of Bob Hope* by Joe Morella, Edward Z. Epstein and Eleanor Clark. Entering a ward of wounded, he'd call out: 'Did you see our show or were you sick before?' And when he saw a room full of GIs in traction: 'Okay, fellas. Don't get up!' Only Hope could get away with such banter. At the same time he would collect letters and personal messages from the troops and support service units for distribution to families and friends when he got back home.

He was on the move all the time. His first United Service Organization (USO) tour was to the UK, where he stayed for five weeks. Then he spent four further weeks in North Africa and Sicily, coming close to the action around Palermo, sharing the dangers with Frances Langford, Tony Romano and Jack Pepper (who had replaced Colonna because of the latter's previous commitments). They were caught up in a surprise night raid by German bombers, their hotel being close to Palermo docks. Bob said later that the noise was deafening and he was never more frightened in his life. After Sicily, the troupe headed back to Algiers, straight into another heavy raid. Bad weather in Iceland on their way home delayed them for a day. They were all exhausted and could have done with the rest. Instead Bob agreed to do a couple of shows for the troops stationed there and then added a third for good measure.

In the eleven weeks they were away, Bob and the others covered some 20,000 miles and gave 250 shows. *Time* magazine called him 'an American folk figure'.

His commitment to Allied servicemen and women became near to an obsession, taking precedence over family, friends and anything remotely accepted as a normal way of life, even in wartime. From the start of their marriage Dolores had had to get used to her husband being away a lot, but in those earlier years she would travel with him at times. She was now used to his being away for long stretches, entertaining the forces.

As he relaxed, with victory in Europe and then against Japan, American troops still stationed abroad consumed his time and energies.

In 1948 he was in Berlin, where American forces were stationed as part of the Allied army of occupation. These were the days of the Berlin air-lift, with East-West relations at a critically low ebb as the Russians blockaded West Berlin. This time Dolores shared the dangers of the 'air corridor' to be part of the entertainment package, along with songwriter Irving Berlin, actress Jane Harvey, Tony Romano and a troupe of dancing girls. Never known to miss an opportunity, Bob suggested he do his regular radio broadcast from Berlin. The entire tour was an enormous hit, with shows in Wiesbaden, Nuremburg and Frankfurt, as well as Berlin.

Problems in South-East Asia continued after the declaration of peace, and in 1954 the country of Vietnam was divided along the 17th parallel. The Communist North became a Soviet client state, the South increasingly under Western influence. French withdrawal from South Vietnam in 1956 was the signal for the North to begin a period of 'destabilization'. This brought US intervention, and the bitter struggle that followed continued until American withdrawal in 1973.

Bob went to Vietnam for the first time in 1964 and dropped the final curtain on these exhaustive and memorable pilgrimages in 1972. They had by then developed into such exciting entertainment spectaculars that he took a team of no fewer than seventy-five people with him on his final tour, with Dolores sharing probably the most emotionally charged two weeks of his long career. Even then he continued for a while to dedicate his Christmases to the cause, visiting military hospitals in Vietnam.

It was a long time since he could call Christmas his own. It had begun in 1948, with an emergency call to hit the entertainment trail for the sake of service morale while he was preparing for a traditional Christmas celebration with his wife and family. He was soon visiting war zones all over the world in an astonishing demonstration of devotion and self-sacrifice. From Alaska to Europe, island strongholds to Cuba, Korea to Greenland, and of course to Vietnam, he travelled more than a million miles to entertain his beloved GIs. 23,000 miles in thirteen days was no more than par for the course on these Vietnam expeditions.

An emotional moment for Bob came when he attended the Silver Anniversary Dinner of the USO in the International Ballroom of the Washington Hilton in the mid-1960s. Some 1,200 distinguished guests were present, and he was astonished when he was suddenly made aware of a change in the programme, with the dramatic announcement by MC John Daly:

'Ladies and Gentlemen, the President of the United States.'

Lyndon B. Johnson strode in and then proceeded to talk about Hope. He said they were there to honour a man with two unusual traits — an actor who was not running for office (an allusion to Ronald Reagan), and a frequent visitor to Vietnam who had never been asked to testify before the Senate Foreign Relations Committee. He also mentioned the bestselling book which Hope had produced some twenty years before about his travels to entertain the troops in the Second World War, called *I Never Left Home*.

Said Johnson in an amusing and witty speech: 'Since then he has spent so much time with our troops overseas that there are those who now say he ought to write a sequel. He could call this one, *I Never Came Back*. Bob, we are very glad that you came back long enough to be with us tonight . . . when the USO was founded twenty-five years ago, Bob was there, and he is here tonight.' And then: 'This plaque is to Bob Hope and says: "Thanks for the Memory from a grateful nation".'

In response, Bob was on top form. He gagged about the President, the evening's master of ceremonies, golfing (of course) and the occasion ('. . . the USO and I have been going steady for twenty-five years . . . it's the nicest travel agency I've ever had. They handle more actors than the Republican Party'). And about the USO again: 'It's done a lot for me. How else would I be able to go on trips with gals like Lana Turner, Jayne Mansfield, Janis Paige, Carroll Baker and Anita Bryant, and have my wife pack my lunch?'

Bob always made a big deal out of the beautiful girls who went with him on his USO tours, and his 'traditional' attitude towards them was later to be a target for the growing feminist lobby. His views on girls were simple and direct and never changed over the years. They also brought him a lot of laughs, as they did that night at the USO Anniversary Dinner: 'Of course, some people don't think the USO should send pretty girls overseas because they get the fellows too excited. I think that's ridiculous. I think the fellows should see what they're fighting for.'

It was always part of his special therapy for the serving men overseas to take along girls and glamour. His pointed jokes, the wolf-whistles and calls of delight from the audience, the autographs, occasional kiss and hug from the girls and their nearness to guys who hadn't seen a girl in months made up the simple yet effective formula which registered his shows so strongly with serving men.

Then on to Martha Raye, who was often the subject of his gags: 'And I want to tell you that Martha Raye did a marvellous job. She really had a ball. She couldn't do enough for the boys.' In fact, he admired Martha Raye enormously, as he did most of those he used to poke fun at during his performances. One of the funniest two-liners perhaps and certainly one of the most cutting was delivered at Martha's expense. She was particularly dedicated to her wartime tours overseas, and Bob talks about bumping into her in Vietnam: 'At first I thought Martha was wounded; then I realized she had her mouth open.'

Just before Christmas that year (1965) Bob was on his way to Vietnam for the second time. There were sixty-three in the contingent this time, plus masses of equipment including props, lighting and scenery, not forgetting Bob's stock of giant 'idiot cards' with their three-inch-tall letters. (He had long since given up using any form of teleprompter, with which he had never been comfortable.) In the party on this trip were Anita Bryant, Kaye Stevens, Jerry Colonna, of course, Les Brown and his band, Jack Jones, Carroll Baker, the Nicholas Brothers, Diana Lynn Batts and Joey Heatherton.

Bob has often said, not surprisingly, that these USO shows in distant lands were among the most emotional, satisfying, exciting, difficult and uncomfortable of his entire career. At times in Vietnam the team performed very close to Viet Cong positions, and it says much for those who went with him, including the girls, that never was there any talk of not putting on a show because of the dangers.

Bob talks of one particular incident in Vietnam when they were warned they were in a position which regularly drew sniper fire. Before the show started, a sergeant-major took the microphone for a pointed announcement about what was to be done in case of a mortar attack. He wanted the aisles kept clear on both sides of the stage, the left-side audience would move to the left, the right side to the right, the centre section to the rear and — 'The Bob Hope Show will take over in those cosy foxholes immediately adjacent to the stage.'

Once in Vietnam the hotel Bob was booked into was blown up by the Viet Cong ten minutes before he was due to arrive. American intelligence later discovered that the bomb had been meant to kill him and crush morale.

The tensions were often enormous, the situations frightening for civilians, and always the schedules were punishing as Bob took every opportunity to bring his entertainment package to as many servicemen as possible, crowding in as many shows as he could.

Hazardous flights in military planes and moving from one battle zone to another would be pushed into a day which could start at 7 a.m. and include shows in both locations. Now over sixty, he tired more easily but he still had the energy, drive and positive temperament more fitting to a man twenty years younger. Always, the gags when on stage came over fresh and fluent, timed to perfection, and with that jaunty cockiness which had become such a trademark of the world's greatest comedian: 'I didn't believe there were any sharks — till I found out there were 3,000 GIs here named Shorty' and, 'Don't believe it when they tell you that sharks will eat anything. We threw Colonna in, and they threw him back.'

The Vietnam trip in 1965 covered 23,000 miles in twelve days, and Bob and his team put on twenty-five shows. They came back with 150,000 feet of film which had to be cut down to just 9,000 feet for Hope's televised show. Eighteen technicians wrestled for a couple of weeks with this thankless job, because so much wonderful film had to be left out. Bob applied some fine tuning an1 added a commentary to a finale which he felt was better than all the rest of the programme. It was made up of all kinds of interesting, fascinating, humorous, emotional, happy, silly shots of servicemen, taken generally when they weren't aware that the camera was on them. It was *Candid Camera,* Bob Hope version, ahead of its time.

In his book *Five Women I Love,* Bob explains it like this: 'My favourite part of the show is what we call "The Tribute" . . . it shows the men in various unguarded moments, in times of stress, when they're relaxed and laughing, when they're praying, when they're working and when they're fighting . . . like the shot of a GI perched in a tree and sipping a beer, or a soldier with both legs in traction, laughing happily as Carroll Baker kisses him, or a flight of jets screaming off a carrier into action.'

These were happy, buoyant, vivid days for Hope. He was a national hero. For the remainder of the 1960s he continued his triumphant annual march into Vietnam. But times were changing. As the war dragged on with no sign of victory, the American people became disillusioned, restless and then aggressive in their attitudes and their condemnation of the war which seemed to have no end and which, for increasing numbers, was of diminishing relevance. The sharply felt sense of patriotism which at first puffed out America's national chest with pride, as the GIs went into battle as the sole saviour of the Free World from Communism, couldn't be maintained for ever. As the call to 'bring our boys home' grew, urged on by a strong political and feminist lobby, Bob's expeditions to entertain the troops became a target for the 'anti' faction and in a sense a symbol, however inaccurate, of the political-military hierarchy whose rooted bigotry allowed no consideration of withdrawal without victory.

Bob had strong feelings about the Vietnam issue and, with typical candour, did not hide them. He considered military action right as a means of sorting out the Viet Cong problem, going so far as to state that if the military had been left to get on with the job unhampered, the war would have been over in three weeks, and three million lives would have been saved.

In many ways a traditionalist, Bob Hope was seen by some as being too willing to toe the official line. He was resented, through the implication and association of his concerts for servicemen in action, for what was seen by his opponents as support for White House policies. Yet he felt genuinely that in Vietnam there was a dangerous situation which the United States had to deal with and was equally sincere that compromise or appeasement in any form would simply permit the growth of local misery and injustice. It is probably fair to say that, when America first went in to Vietnam, the majority of Americans felt the same way. It was only when the United States became deadlocked in a battle which seemed never-ending, with casualties mounting, that the anti-war lobby began to articulate the view of an increasing number of American people. Hope's concerts for the armed forces seemed increasingly in opposition to the growing movement which was demanding peace. His own, perhaps simplistic, views on the use and results of armed intervention did not help matters, nor his close and cosy relationship with the President.

But for all that, Bob Hope continued to be widely respected and genuinely liked as a performer and a man. For the majority of his hundreds of thousands of fans, not least those in the UK, his personal views were his own affair. They admired and loved him as an entertainer and laughter-maker supreme.

Bob's views did not change over the years. His comments, widely reported, were sometimes unwise and indiscreet and did nothing to clarify his own position — which was simply that, while troops were fighting in Vietnam, they needed to be entertained from time to time. However, he distorted that issue and allowed himself to be exploited by advocates of a withdrawal with some frank and uncompromising statements which showed without doubt which side he was on. A staunch anti-Communist, he declared: 'Don't let anyone kid you about why we're in Vietnam. If we weren't, those Commies would have the whole thing and it wouldn't be long until we'd be looking at them off the coast of Santa Monica.' Even more radical was: 'You just have to let them know you're boss and come in and bomb Hanoi and clear it out and they would say, "Where do we sign?"' Also reckless, even though put across as a joke, was: 'Bombing Hanoi is the best slum-clearance programme they ever had.'

Bob's well-publicized friendship with Spiro Agnew, one-time Republican nominee for the vice-presidency, and his cordial relations with the presidential office, the White House establishment and the military, all became good fodder for the anti-Hope campaigners, who branded him a 'political hawk'. It hurt him deeply.

In 1971 he was set to receive the New York City Council of Churches' 'Family of Man' prize but under pressure from a group of activist young clergymen the decision was reassessed and the award withdrawn. But he stuck to his convictions: 'I'm not in favour of any war,' he said, 'but I'm also not in favour of surrender. We're helping people maintain their freedom.'

The growing anti-war mood was beginning to have a serious impact towards the end of 1967. The American army was making little progress, casualties were mounting, and as public opinion began vigorously to question and argue the case against a continuation in Vietnam, the USO found for the first time that it wasn't easy to convince celebrities and Hollywood stars that they should be going out to entertain the troops. Raquel Welch went with Hope on his 1967 tour, when his popularity among servicemen was still vast and he was acclaimed with customary enthusiasm.

The call for a withdrawal of American troops from Vietnam was growing ever stronger. Earlier that year, some 50,000 Vietnam protestors had marched through the streets of Washington, and the administration was having to take notice. Lyndon Johnson, doubtless wearied by the tribulations of office and in particular the Vietnam question, didn't seek a further term as president, and Richard Nixon took over.

In 1969 Bob Hope maintained much popular appeal: there were more viewers for the January screening of his televised Christmas special than the year before.

During the year the groundswell of public opinion in support of a pull-out of Vietnam at almost any price grew to encompass huge tracts of college campuses at one extreme and significant elements of government administration at the other. Bob found it difficult to understand the view, asserting that a dishonourable withdrawal would do no good for world peace in the long run and would encourage Communism to infiltrate other areas. In 1969 he responded to the situation by extending his Vietnam tour to include other parts of the world, and although in Vietnam he encountered the first signs of dissent, that year's Hope spectacular, shown on television in January 1970, drew the biggest single viewing audience for a non-motion picture or special event in television history.

As troop withdrawals from Vietnam began, he put his standing and publicity machine behind an attempted revival of that year's 4 July Independence Day celebrations as an honest demonstration of faith in America and national unity, a rally which was threatened when some 5,000 hippies had to be dispersed by riot police.

In 1971 he made an astonishing move to help gain the release of some 300 American prisoners of war being held by the Viet Cong. On a personal mission, unsanctioned by the State Department, though with their unofficial backing, he flew to the Laotian capital of Vientiane and talked directly with the First Secretary of the North Vietnamese Embassy, Nguyen Van Thanh, for almost 1½ hours. He wanted to take his company to perform for American prisoners of war, and their eventual return to the United States. And he pledged in return that he would put his energies into trying to raise $10 million for the building of hospitals and schools to aid North Vietnamese children. Although the talks were cordial, nothing resulted.

Most significant in the early 1970s was the change of mood among the GIs themselves. Younger, enlisted soldiers with different values were depressed and had no heart for the fight. Undisciplined, rebellious, politically radical, they became disillusioned and uninterested. Drug-taking had become a major problem, an estimated fifty per cent of gunshot wounds were caused by GIs themselves, not the enemy, and attacks by soldiers on their own officers were of alarming proportions.

Against this background Bob Hope arrived to do his Christmas Day show at Long Binh, near Saigon, in 1971. The ecstasy of earlier years had by now turned to anguish and ugliness. The anti-Vietnam bandwagon had rolled as far as Vietnam itself. Bob was identified with continued support for the war, and some troops were enraged that Jane Fonda, the left-wing campaigner, had not been allowed to tour Vietnam with an anti-war play.

The stadium where Bob was to perform was picketed with 'Peace not Hope' posters carried by soldiers. On stage he was heckled, shouted down, and towards the end scores of soldiers got up and walked out. At one point he was provoked into shouting back at them, for these were not the servicemen he knew from his 1939–45 wartime days, or indeed from the patriotic early years in Vietnam. These youngsters were a different breed, fed on flower-power, sexual liberation, with full-frontal nudity, and a doctrine which put self before country. Against this harsher realism of life, Bob's 'naughty' jokes which hinted ingenuously at sex (like *Miss World America:* 'What would you do if your girlfriend asked you to pay for a new dress?' *Bob Hope:* 'Talk her out of it.') had no meaning. The banner which proclaimed: 'The Vietnam war is a Bob Hope joke' was unkind as well as being unjust, but one thing was certain: the Americans in Vietnam had little stomach to carry on the fight, and soon they would have their way and the war would be over.

When Bob took his company to Vietnam again in 1972, he reckoned it might be the last time and took Dolores with him. With the war drawing to a close, audiences put aside any bitter feelings they may have had and gave him an appreciative and re-sounding reception. It was emotional for Bob as the curtain came down on the tour with a performance for airmen on Guam, with Dolores singing 'White Christmas'. It was his last Christmas show.

7 Big Days at the Box Office

After the enormous success of *Road to Singapore* and *Road to Zanzibar,* Paramount couldn't wait to pull the team together again. The writing wizardry of Frank Butler and Don Hartman was once more applied to the screenplay; *Zanzibar* producer Paul Jones was re-engaged; and this time David Butler replaced Victor Schertzinger as director.

But before Bob, Bing and Dotty set out once more on their skylarking adventures, Hope worked on *My Favourite Blonde,* which Paramount released in March 1942. This new picture cast Bob in the role of Larry Haines, straight man for a trained penguin. Between engagements he encounters Karen Bentley (Madeleine Carroll) on a train. He thinks she is just a gorgeous if scatty blonde, but she is — couldn't you guess? — a beautiful British spy being chased by Nazi agents (played by Gale Sondergaard and George Zucco). The picture consists of Bob, Madeleine and bird being pursued countrywide by road, on a train and in a plane.

The basic story had been put together by two of Bob's former regular radio gag-writers, Melvin Frank and Norman Panama, and the result of everyone's contribution was a well-made, carefully constructed, very funny and very successful picture.

Bob liked it particularly because it didn't restrict him altogether to what he was now famous for — slapstick and double takes. Not that he minded that, but the opportunity for more variety in acting which *My Favourite Blonde* gave him was welcome. It also proved, if any proof was needed, that, despite his public impact as part of the *Road* team, he could still operate successfully on his own. It is curious that, throughout the decade of *Road* films, the public was ready to accept all three main characters individually in other movies and often in very different roles.

For Bob Hope, too, the chance of working with Madeleine

Carroll in *Blonde* was considered something of a prize. She was the archetypal British beauty, classically beautiful, cool, elegant, distinctly mysterious yet with an amazingly innocent, sensual quality. She had achieved a daunting reputation as Hitchcock's icy blonde in *The Thirty Nine Steps* and other important films. Hope commented on her obvious beauty and was not surprisingly impressed by her talent.

The film also gave him plenty of opportunity to promote his screen image of the superficial smart-Alec whose courage evaporates at the first sign of danger; the boyishly audacious lover who never quite has the confidence he needs to win the girl, without a little help from her; the self-effacing, hard-not-to-like reluctant hero. There is also ample opportunity for him to do what many believe he does better than anyone — responding to a line in the film with an out-of-context line far removed from the plot, but which he and his audience relate to instantly. This was a basic feature of the *Road* films and in *Blonde* was continued successfully with such lines as Carroll's: 'Do you know what it feels like to be watched and hounded every second?' alluding to her life as a spy. 'I used to, but now I pay cash for everything,' responds Hope.

Bob believed in exploiting every possible opportunity for promoting his films and shamelessly plugged them to the 20 million fans who listened every week to his radio broadcasts. Thus the build-up for *Blonde* had been going on for quite some time before the film came out, even before it was made. He began by telling listeners how beautiful Madeleine Carroll was, and this was developed until he began to joke about making a film with her. It is said that it was Miss Carroll who suggested they be teamed in a film, though whether as a result of Bob's radio fantasies is not known. But she did telephone him one day to thank him for all the publicity he was giving her and suggesting they do a picture together.

During the production, Bob kept listeners in touch with progress, in the process gaining inestimable publicity value for the film and building up such expectancy that box-office success was assured. 'Madeleine Carroll and I are making a picture called *My Favourite Blonde,*' he'd say. 'She's a spy and keeps chasing me. That's right. Madeleine Carroll keeps chasing me . . . and you think Walt Disney makes fantastic pictures!' Later he would say he was the only man in the country who wanted longer working hours and: 'This morning the producer asked me to study my lines . . . I'm working on a picture with Madeleine Carroll, and he wants me to study *my* lines!'

It was blatant electioneering but nobody seemed to mind. It was good for listening figures, good for the film, good for Madeleine Carroll, and good of course for Bob Hope. Other promotional cameos in the film are the penguin's rendition of Hope's theme tune 'Thanks for the Memory' and the unbilled 'walk-on' appearance of Bing Crosby as a leather-jacketed truck driver. This history-making ploy delighted audiences, and the basic idea was to be used again in Hope pictures.

Road to Morocco, the third film in the series, was released on 5 October, 1942, in a mountain of publicity oversell. America was now fully embroiled in the war, and the picture was welcomed for its outrageous escapism. Billed as 'The Greatest Road Show of 'Em All', *Morocco* has Bing (as Jeff Peters) and Bob (as Turkey Jackson) shipwrecked on a Mediterranean beach. Promotion for the film described Bing as a 'pasha with the accent on the pash', Bob as a 'wolf in sheik's clothing', Lamour as the 'Queen of Araby', and the film itself as 'A Harem-Scarem Riot of Song and Laughter!' It was about right. If anything, underdone! Director David Butler worked cleverly to retain the essential spontaneity, and if he could see something developing he would deliberately let the camera run. He freely admitted later that some of the funniest scenes resulted from this device.

The plot isn't important, but as a matter of documentation it does provide the opportunity for Crosby to sell Hope into slavery in lieu of payment for dinner. He wants to join him when he hears that Hope is now 'owned' by the beautiful Princess Shalimar (played of course by Dorothy Lamour). The villainous Sheik Mullay Kasim (supremely overplayed by Anthony Quinn) gives our heroes plenty of trouble before they manage to escape, and this wild and wacky eighty-three minutes of vintage *Road* ends with Bing and Bob floating on a raft into New York harbour. The film was lavishly produced by Paul Jones. Writers Don Hartman and Frank Butler received an Oscar nomination for their work. A sultry Yvonne De Carlo, who later appeared in exactly the kind of film that *Morocco* spoofed with such outrageousness, was way down the cast list as a nineteen-year-old at the beginning of her film career.

The picture produced another song which was to become a

popular standard. The combined talents of Johnny Burke and Jimmy Van Heusen wrote 'Constantly' and 'Ain't Got a Dime to my Name' especially for the film, but it was their third composition that was to stand the test of time as well as becoming a hit tune of the day, as Bing crooned 'Moonlight Becomes You' to the beautiful Miss Lamour.

Two legendary stories from this phenomenally successful film concerned animals — a camel in one instance and horses in another.

Early on in the film Bob and Bing are sneaked up on from behind, each being given a lick on the cheek by the camel. The intended gag was that each should think the other had kissed him, but unscheduled events boosted the scene into what became generally accepted as one of the funniest sequences in any of the *Road* films. After the camel had kissed Bob, it spat in his face. Hope staggered backwards, Crosby collapsed into laughter, as indeed did most of the set, and Butler inspiringly captured the whole sequence on film. Bob said he expected Butler to order another take, but Dave replied: 'No, that's all.' Whenever asked about the incident in the years that followed, Butler insisted that he'd worked for months getting the camel to respond to direction.

The other incident was when Bob and Bing were being chased through the Casbah by Arabian horsemen. Popular cowboy star Ken Maynard had been drafted in to help with the scene, but, came the action and, as Bob explained later, 'Ken led his horsemen like it was the first furlong of the Kentucky Derby.' At the time though, it was a serious thing and Bob and Bing were not amused. Somehow the horses had been cued into action before they had expected them and they literally had to fling themselves out of the way. When they later stormed at Butler, who had once been a stuntman, complaining how near to disaster they had come, he apparently was laughing almost uncontrollably, in between times managing to gasp ...! 'Yeah, how about that? We got a great shot.' According to Hope, Bing insisted: 'Great shot? You almost killed Bob and me.' Dave responded: 'Oh, I wouldn't do that. Not until the final scene anyway.'

For *Star Spangled Rhythm,* a morale-boosting film designed principally to entertain the armed forces, released in December 1942, Bob appears as master of ceremonies at a sailors' entertainment. The picture includes as many of Paramount's famous stars as possible in a story about a sailor, played by Eddie Bracken, visiting Hollywood to see his father (played by Victor Moore), who has told him that he runs the studio but in reality is only the gate man. The studio switchboard operator (played by Betty Hutton) helps the innocent deception along, with the aid of the studio's stars. Ray Milland, Mary Martin, Veronica Lake, Fred MacMurray, Dorothy Lamour, Alan Ladd, Dick Powell, Franchot Tone, Paulette Goddard, William Bendix and Susan Hayward are among the now legendary Hollywood names to be seen in the film, which also boosted such Johnny Mercer-Harold Arlen songs as 'Let's Hit the Road to Dreamland' and, in particular, 'That Old Black Magic'.

Other Bob Hope films around this time were *They Got Me Covered* and *The Princess and the Pirate,* through the Sam Goldwyn connection mentioned earlier, and in 1943 he appeared with Betty Hutton and ZaSu Pitts in Paramount's *Let's Face It.* The screenplay was by Harry Tugend from the 1925 successful Broadway comedy *The Cradle Snatchers,* which had already been made into a film by Twentieth Century Fox in 1927. It appeared under its new title as a hit musical on stage in 1941 with music by Dorothy Fields and Cole Porter and with Danny Kaye in his first starring role, but this latest version, despite Hope's presence, was not well received.

The story centres on three wives out for revenge on wayward husbands. They hire three soldiers as gigolos, but complications arise when the soldiers' girlfriends find out. The wives are played by Eve Arden, ZaSu Pitts and Phyllis Povah, the soldiers by Hope, Dave Willock and Cully Richards. Betty Hutton, Dona Drake and Marjorie Weaver are the girlfriends. One report suggested that it 'offered more noise than wit and had too many characters running around'. It is certainly one of the most forgettable and least successful and significant of the Hope pictures from this period.

The early 1940s, as we have noted, was the time when Bob fought the studio for more money for himself out of movie-making, even though his gross income from entertainment sources alone in 1940 was said to be well in excess of $450,000. His determined opposition to Paramount meant he didn't make a film for nearly a year, but that didn't mean he was inactive. Radio, personal appearances and the first USO tours occupied him so fully during the 1940s that he might well have wondered how on earth he ever managed the time to make pictures.

There are plenty of Hope fans who will tell you that *Road to Utopia* was the funniest movie in the series. In a number of ways it did rather cleverly extend the basic formula. It was the first *Road* film to be scripted by radio gag-writers and not surprisingly depended more heavily on verbal joking. It was a period picture, which the others had not been. It also made much more use of gags and devices which were totally disconnected from the movement of the plot and which, despite the vintage character of the film, were very up to date and instantly recognizable to cinema audiences. Again it was a huge success at the box office.

There hadn't been a *Road* film for more than two years. Some reports suggested that this was because of Paramount's astute policy in spacing out the pictures to avoid the public's tiring of them too quickly. It is true that, although the picture was finished early 1944, it wasn't released until the following year, but so many films were being made at around that time that there was certainly a queue to get them out on release. It is also possible that *Utopia* was held back because of Crosby's *Going My Way,* released by Paramount in 1944 and strongly rumoured for an Oscar nomination.

Road to Utopia emerged when two of Hope's young gag-writers, Norman Panama and Melvin Frank, concocted a Klondike adventure about a couple of vaudevillian con men who travel to Alaska in search of gold. Paul Jones, who had produced *Road to Zanzibar,* was back in charge of production, and Hal Walker, who had learned film direction assisting Victor Schertzinger (who had directed the first two *Road* pictures before dying unexpectedly in his sleep), took over for the first time as director. Bob played the part of Chester Hooton, Bing was Duke Johnson, and Dorothy Lamour was Sal.

Utopia was the first *Road* film not written by Hartman and Butler, and there was some anxiety about that. There was some concern, too, about one or two of the stunts, which were more outrageous than anything attempted before or after in the *Road* films, and over the controversial ending which raised official eyebrows over a moral issue which at that time was by no means certain to pass the censor.

Hope, Crosby and Lamour were such big stars at the time that even though the picture was under the control of Paramount, Panama and Frank felt obliged to 'sell' their idea to them individually if they were to stand any chance of having the story accepted by the studio. The film was different in a number of ways for a *Road* opus. For one thing it was shot as a flashback and additionally used Robert Benchley periodically as a dry-humoured narrator, whose face popped up from time to time filling a 'cut-in' circle in a corner of the screen. The picture also provided Hope with one of the most famous lines in cinema history, to run alongside Humphrey Bogart's purported utterance in *Casablanca*. Our two heroes enter a rough Yukon saloon and playing up their tough-guy image, Bing orders a couple of fingers of rotgut. When bartender villain Douglass Dumbrille gruffly turns to Hope and intimidatingly asks what he wants, Bob asks meekly for a glass of lemonade . . . then adding, knowingly, 'In a dirty glass!' It is said to be Bob's favourite line from the picture and is certainly the most famous. It has since been written into the folklore not just of the *Road* films but of Hollywood movie-making in general.

Road to Utopia also veered away from the accepted tradition by giving Lamour to Hope at the end, even if by default. The final scene of the flashback, which takes up most of the film, sees our intrepid trio on an ice-floe being pursued by villains in a race to find an Alaskan gold mine. Sal (Dotty) loves Duke Johnson (Bing), but the two are separated when a crack appears in the ice and Duke drifts away on his own, leaving Chester Hooton (Bob) and Sal together. The movie ends in the supposed present, some thirty years on, with Bob and Dotty grey and ageing. The two had married once Dotty had given up all hope of Bing returning. They are sitting quietly at home, in front of the fire, when there is someone at the door and, surprise, surprise, it's long-lost Bing, who obviously made his escape from his pursuers after all. The film's outrageous pay-off comes when Bob and Dotty introduce their son to Bing, for he is the image of him. There were real doubts that the censor would pass the sequence. Perhaps Hope's telling end-of-shot line helped. He shrugged his shoulders and said: 'We adopted.'

The film also introduced what was to become another Crosby-Hope special, the 'Put it there, pal' routine, and delighted audiences with sequences involving a tame bear. Typical of the Hope humour at that time was when he cuddles up to the grizzly believing it to be Lamour. Patting a paw, he remarks; 'Dear, you've been working too hard.'

Neither Hope nor Crosby was pleased at working with the bear, and their mistrust of it was justified. In one scene, which had gone well in rehearsal, the bear showed signs of being self-willed and Bing and Bob had to remain motionless while the trainer came on the set and struggled to control the animal. Both said they wouldn't work with the animal again. The very next day it savaged the arm of its trainer.

As usual there was a lot of skylarking on the set, and Dorothy Lamour once again had her patience and tolerance stretched. One day their thoughtlessness became too much. Dotty had to be at the studio at six o'clock to be corseted and costumed for a scene scheduled to start at nine. There was no sign of Crosby or Hope, and they still hadn't shown up by lunchtime. Dotty got out of her elaborate costume, had lunch, struggled back into it again and returned to the set. Still no sign of Hope and Crosby. They had simply gone off for a day's golfing and hadn't bothered to tell anyone. With no message concerning their whereabouts, the early joky atmosphere on the set began to wear thin. Finally, towards the end of the afternoon, furious and uncomfortable at being trussed up all day, Dotty stormed off the set. Shortly after, Bob and Bing showed up, full of apologies and claiming they had forgotten all about the scene they had to do.

The studio top brass then phoned through to Dotty's dressing-room wanting to know why she wasn't on set ready. She explained what had happened and outlined just how long it would now take her to get back into all her costume and make-up. According to Dotty, they fully understood.

Said Lamour later about the incident: 'The next day all was patched up. Of course, Bing and Bob took turns teasing the life out of me, calling me "that temperamental Lamour woman who stormed off the set", but they didn't pull another stunt like that ever again.'

Perhaps the best features of *Road to Utopia* were the contemporary references and gags which cleverly infiltrated the scenario, totally out of context. When Hope and Crosby do badly at a talent contest, Hope murmurs: 'Next time I'll bring Sinatra.' At another point they are heaving coal into a ship's boiler when a man strides across the scene in full evening dress. Asked if he is in the picture, he says he isn't. 'I'm just taking a short cut to stage ten,' he mutters, and walks on. The *Road* pictures were by now a cinema phenomenon.

Bob was also busy presiding over the Motion Picture Academy Awards ceremony, starring in radio specials, golfing with Bing and others in tournaments and, as the war in Europe drew to a close, taking a troupe over to Britain and then into France and Germany entertaining the forces.

Although the next *Road* film was a long time coming, he did make pictures — *Monsieur Beaucaire* (released in September 1946), *My Favourite Brunette* in April 1947, *Variety Girl* in August 1947 and later that year *Where There's Life,* for in the meantime he had won his long and bitter battle with Paramount and formed Hope Enterprises, enabling him to make a set number of pictures a year working with the studio on a co-operative basis. His dogged and eventually successful stand on what he felt was an important principle was to lead to the break-up of the hitherto all-powerful studio system and the liberalization of the relationship between studio and star in all kinds of ways.

It was Paramount producer Sol Siegel who had the idea of casting Bob Hope in a riotous burlesque of Booth Tarkington's *Monsieur Beaucaire,* and he had Norman Panama and Mel Frank working on the script while Hope was still away from home, giving priority to troop entertainment.

When Paul Jones later took over as producer and saw what Panama and Frank had written, he wasn't impressed and called in another writer, without notifying the Writers Guild, which he was required to do. Hope said later that, although all this happened while he was in Europe, he understood that Panama and Frank were furious when they discovered what had happened, and refused to submit the remainder of the script, even though the final thirty pages of the ninety-page scenario had been completed. An agreement was finally reached with intervention at the highest level in the form of Paramount top executive Henry Ginsberg. Panama and Frank left their script with Paramount and departed.

Director George Marshall had done a good job with the words, but when Hope arrived and saw the preview, he felt it needed some attention and engaged cartoonist-turned-screenwriter Frank Tashlin to give it more visual appeal, especially in the spoof duelling scene. It was exactly what the picture required and that particular sequence became the all-action highlight of a highly successful movie, counted by many critics among Hope's best. The strong supporting cast included Joan Caulfield, Patric Knowles, Marjorie Reynolds and our old friend from *Utopia*, Douglass Dumbrille, but the outrageous plot interpretation was the real star, along with Hope.

Bob plays a barber at the Court of Louis XV and becomes involved in all manner of royal intrigues. At one point he is sentenced to the guillotine and at another is sent on what is supposed to be a fatal mission, posing as the French ambassador to Spain. The story bore little resemblance to the Rudolph Valentino straight version put out by Paramount back in 1924, but it was another major box-office hit for Hope and showed how well he could play a costumed comedy adventure. There were plenty of one- and two-liners to spice up the script.

Hope's first film under the banner of Hope Enterprises was *My Favourite Brunette* in which again he was teamed with Dorothy Lamour.

Dotty, married to Bill Howard, had recently had their first child, a particularly happy event because, some time before, she had been told that, because of an accident while she had been filming *Typhoon,* it was unlikely that she would be able to have a baby. She hadn't worked for six months after the birth of her son, Ridge, and was keen to get started on the new mystery-thriller, which also co-starred those traditional villains Peter Lorre and Lon Chaney Jr.

Said Dorothy: 'The first day of shooting I played the proud Mama, holding Ridge up and showing off to my pals on the set. Ridge was laughing, trying to hold everyone's finger, and doing all those things that babies do to make grown men love them. Lorre and Chaney both came over to play.' Dorothy went on to explain that when 'Uncle Bob' came over, he spoke to Ridge, who immediately stopped laughing and began to scream his head off. 'See,' cracked Bob. 'Lorre and Chaney don't scare the kid. But I sure can!' Bob and Dolores had celebrated the birth of Dorothy's son by presenting the family with a beautiful British-built pram.

In the film Bob takes the part of Ronnie Jackson, waiting to go to the gas chamber in San Quentin prison. He is telling the story to the Press, which leads into a flashback in which the audience see how, as an innocent photographer with an ambition to be a private eye, he became entangled with the affairs of the authentic private detective who worked next door and became one himself in trying to help the mysterious and attractive Carlotta Montay played by Dorothy Lamour. After much chasing, he was menaced and framed by mobsters for the killing of a government official. After the flashback he is given an eleventh-hour reprieve.

The story is reasonably plausible for a Hope movie, but the script by Edmund Beloin and Jack Rose generates plenty of laughs from start to finish, with Hope in an outrageous burlesque of the long-coated private eye so much a popular hero in early post-war movies Alan Ladd catches audiences unawares in a surprise walk-on bit part, and when Bob escapes being executed at the fade-out, it is much to the disappointment of the executioner, who turns out to be Bing Crosby in another guest spot. Says Hope to close the picture: 'He'll take any kind of part.'

It was Bob's idea to have Crosby play the twenty-second scene, and it cost him $25,000, the fee demanded by Crosby for a charity.

Bob gave the film a well-publicized send-off by plugging it on his regular weekly radio show. An astute publicist had the brilliant idea of running a competition, listeners being invited to write in to explain why they would like the première of *My Favourite Brunette* to be held in their living-room. It brought in thousands of entries and directed enormous attention to the film.

A gala première in aid of cancer research launched the film, with Hope as MC of a star-studded show which included the likes of Gene Kelly, Burns and Allen, the Andrews Sisters, Frank Sinatra, Betty Hutton, Dinah Shore, Eddie Cantor, Jimmy Durante, Al Jolson and, of course, Bob's faithful sidekick, Jerry Colonna. The show had widespread radio coverage, going to servicemen and women round the world by means of Armed Forces Radio, and part of it was televised over ABC's Pacific Coast network.

Early in 1946 he was back at Paramount, on the road again with Crosby and Lamour. The picture was something of a surprise. At the time of *Road to Utopia,* while Paramount were waiting to put the film out on release, the studio had announced that *Utopia* would be the final *Road* picture. The news brought howls of protest. Paramount received more than 75,000 letters pleading that the series be continued. Faced with such an overwhelming and unexpected response, the studio rushed out a second announcement, explaining that they were considering another *Road* picture, possibly about a couple of GIs returning home after the war. Likely title: *Road to Home.* It never materialized.

As time advanced, it seemed that Bing, Bob and Dotty had really come to the end of the road. A major problem was their individual schedules and commitments. It must have been a nightmare trying to get them all together at the same time. This was the reason given for the original announcement about the series ending. But there was still some road to travel and eventually *The Road to Rio* began shooting.

There was less fooling around from Hope and Crosby this time. Like Bob, Bing now had his own company, and the picture was a three-cornered deal, with Hope, Crosby and Paramount each owning one third. They each put in about a million dollars, but it was to prove a good investment, Dorothy Lamour, though still a Paramount employee, was said to be hurt when she heard about it. 'They could have considered a four-way split, but no one asked me,' she responded. The story goes that in the end they gave Dotty a tiny percentage, and when the film was coming to the end of its natural life she received a cheque for residual earnings for just 16 cents. To make the point about how much she might have earned, she had it framed!

This fifth film in the hit series was very much the formula as before, but the antics and stunts which had steadily been gaining momentum were held in tighter check in this latest epic. It relied more than its predecessors on straight comedy and had plenty of music, with the Andrews Sisters introduced as a commercial bonus. Their records with Bing had sold more than 5 million copies.

Bob (Hot Lips Barton) and Bing (Scat Sweeney) are on the run, because of a fire they were wrongly blamed for. They hop on a boat bound for Rio de Janeiro and find the gorgeous Lucia Maria de Andrade on board, played of course by Dorothy Lamour. Jerry Colonna plays, of all things, a cavalry captain. Our heroes can't understand why Lamour blows hot and cold with their emotions, but she is being hypnotized by her wicked aunt who wants her to marry a Brazilian she dislikes. There is plenty of action in this *Road* film, which again was a major hit at the box office.

Despite her disappointment at not being included in the financial deal for the picture, Dotty had a great affection for Crosby and Hope, and said she would be hurt if they were to contemplate a *Road* picture without her. It was to happen, but not yet, and on the set of *Rio* there was still plenty of fun for the three of them, even if time-wasting had been cut to a minimum.

By now Dotty knew how to deal with their pranks. At one point, when she had to wear a gown which showed quite a lot of cleavage, Bob kept teasing her and she finally got quite embarrassed about it, which made her fluff her lines. Frustrated, she yelled out: 'Stop everything until Mr Hope has had a good look.'

Road to Rio had queued to get out on release. Bob's next film was delayed also. *The Paleface* brought him together with one of the film world's sexiest and most seductive actresses, the well-endowed Jane Russell. The film itself was good, but commercially it benefited enormously from the huge success of one of the songs from the film, 'Buttons and Bows', with words and music by Jay Livingston and Ray Evans, studio contract songwriters who had worked with Bob on *Monsieur Beaucaire.*

Because the film was a long time going out on release, the song came out ahead of the picture. Bob explained: 'I'm convinced that this had a great deal to do with the immense success of *The Paleface.* ''Buttons and Bows'' had been the number one song on the Hit Parade for several weeks when the film opened at the Paramount Theatre in New York. The song got as much billing as Jane and I did.'

There was a curious sequence of events related to 'Buttons and Bows'. In the film Bob needed a song to sing to Jane Russell while he was driving a wagon and she was sitting in the back. The first effort of Livingston and Evans was discarded, so they got to work again. They were looking for something bouncy, like 'Kansas City' from *Oklahoma.* Ray got things moving in the right direction when he suggested 'Buttons and Bows' as the title. All that was needed now was the song and the lyrics to go with it. It took several weeks before the tune and words emerged, and the film took even longer to see the light of day.

The Paleface was almost a year waiting to be released from the production chaos at Paramount. In the meantime the song was there, ready to be played and sung. Livingston and Evans played it to Dinah Shore and she liked it. With just eight musicians improvising a backing, the record was cut literally minutes before a midnight deadline for the start of a musicians' strike which would shut down all recording. Hope later recorded the song and later still had parody lyrics written by Livingston and Evans which he used for personal appearances for many years.

'Buttons and Bows' received an Oscar for the best movie song of 1948 and, helped by the song, *The Paleface* became Bob's biggest-ever earner. It grossed a phenomenal $7 million and rocketed him to the top of the Hollywood popularity stakes. The recognition was fully deserved, for *The Paleface* was an excellent film and won its share of critical acclaim. It was different from the *Road* pictures, relying less heavily on quick-fire jokes tumbling one after another in rapid succession.

Bob is well cast as the bumbling, fumbling Painless Peter Potter, a dentist, who marries Calamity Jane, played by Jane Russell — who incidentally was second choice. Ginger Rogers was said to have been offered the part, but wanted more money to do it, a mere $325,000 plus a percentage! Russell, keen to live down or perhaps capitalize on the instant fame that came from her début in *The Outlaw,* was less fussy.

Billed in the earlier Howard Hughes Western as 'mean, moody, magnificent' with her ample curves and provocative (for the times) 'bed scene' with co-star Jack Buetel, she was eager to swing away from at least some of the legend which had already built up around her. She performed well in the spoof Western with Hope and was an excellent foil, demonstrating with due credit her talent as a comedienne as she satirized her own sultry, sex-siren image against Hope as the cowardly comic, braggard and lecher.

The successful box office of *The Paleface* made a sequel an automatic reaction for all concerned, but not until four years later (in 1952) did *Son of Paleface* emerge. Hope's diary at this time was fuller than a Tokyo underground train during the rush hour. But somehow Paramount managed to pin him down long enough for them to be able to release two more films in 1949, one in 1950 and another two in 1951.

In *Sorrowful Jones* he took his first semi-serious role in a remake of the 1934 hit which had starred Shirley Temple, *Little Miss Marker.* It cast him as Sorrowful Jones, with Lucille Ball for the first time, in the basic Damon Runyon story cleverly angled for his particular talent by scriptwriter Jack Rose. Bob enjoyed doing the film and described it as memorable because it took him out of a hundred per cent comedy and because it was his first picture with Lucille Ball. He was also predisposed to it because he was fond of Damon Runyon. 'I got to know him when we lived at the same hotel in New York, back in the early 1930s. And his rave for ''Thanks for the Memory'' in *The Big Broadcast of 1938* had saved my movie career,' he said.

The story is about a street-hard bookie (Bob) who becomes guardian to a gambler's little daughter, at the same time getting involved with race-track rackets and mean crooks. The picture blends sentiment with cynicism, and on the whole Bob made a good job of the acting, generally standing up well to the critics' gaze in touching scenes with little Mary Jane Saunders, who took the part first played by Shirley Temple and who inevitably, by comparison, couldn't ever be expected to replace her.

Bob's other film to be released in 1949 was *The Great Lover,* which co-starred him with Rhonda Fleming. A title like that gave him plenty of opportunity for pointed gags, and he didn't waste the chance. 'She was surprised that we did our love scenes so fast,' quipped Bob. 'They didn't have to stop to give me adrenalin shots.' And: 'Rhonda was a sweet girl, but I think she had *The Great Lover* mixed up with my previous picture. Whenever I asked her how I was doing in the love scenes, she said ''Sorrowful''.' Nor could he resist a jibe against his old adversary, Crosby. He jested about Rhonda's making a come-back. 'She's just done a picture with Crosby,' he said.

The picture was funny without being spectacular, but it did well at the box office. A transatlantic liner is the setting, and Bob is a scoutmaster who becomes involved with unscrupulous card-players and a penniless duke who has a beautiful daughter (Rhonda Fleming), and somehow he manages to capture a murderer. Distinguished actors Roland Young and Roland Culver give excellent support.

Fancy Pants, released in 1950, cast Bob once more with Lucille Ball. Both stars had received some critical acclaim for their performances in *Sorrowful Jones,* and Bob was delighted that, despite the instinctive and almost inevitable acceptance by critics and public alike of him only as a comedian, his acting ability in *Sorrowful Jones* had been noticed. 'Working in the picture gave me the chance to do something serious without being too obvious,' he commented. In *Fancy Pants* he plays a British actor in need of cash who agrees to be butler to a small-town American family, the arrangement allowing the family to do some social climbing among their friends. Ball plays the daughter of the house —

'always fun and games to work with', said Bob.

One scene brought him near to disaster, however. Ball was supposed to be teaching him to ride, on a kind of wooden barrel which had been rigged up by the studio so that it would buck and roll, adding essential realism to the scene. Bob was unhappy about the contraption, which was some seven feet off the ground, and was soon in trouble after being hitched up onto it. He slipped and fell off the side, where he lay spread-eagled on the cement floor. He couldn't move. An ambulance was summoned and he was rushed to the nearby Presbyterian Hospital in Hollywood where for a while doctors feared he might be paralysed. Fortunately, severe bruising was the worst problem, but he was in hospital for a week.

It wasn't the most comfortable of his pictures. He has recalled how both a real horse and then Bruce Cabot, who was appearing in the film with him, stepped on his feet, an incident which eight years later resulted in the need for minor surgery.

During these post-war years most of the major film theatres were still booking stage shows, and Bob Hope was always eager to return to his first and abiding love, the stage. As the ratings for his radio show began to sag and he was urged to freshen the format for a new post-war audience, he found consolation in taking the show cast 'on the road'. Another incentive was the warm public response to the prospect of seeing him in person. A thirty-six-centre whirlwind tour, embarked upon shortly after his Berlin airlift adventure, and shared with singer Doris Day and bandleader Les Brown, netted him $700,000, which worked out at a massive $11,000 a day!

His tax bill was said to be prodigious, and it was claimed that much of the money he earned went straight to the government.

Bob also began reluctantly to sharpen his interest in television, continued to have a full programme of benefit appearances and was constantly in demand as the country's greatest and most popular MC. But during this period pictures were still the 'steady markers' for his international public, and Paramount, surprised and impressed by the standard of his straight acting in *Sorrowful Jones,* took inspiration from another Damon Runyon story and put him in the *Lemon Drop Kid,* released in 1951.

Here he worked with Marilyn Maxwell. It was their first film together, though she toured with him on a number of occasions.

The picture was a blatant attempt to re-run the success of *Sorrowful Jones,* but it didn't quite make it and had more than its share of problems before it finally went out on release.

Bob is the 'Lemon Drop Kid', a race-track tout who finds himself having to raise $10,000 by Christmas. His life depends on it. Marilyn Maxwell, a good-looking blonde with a flair for the comedy line and tipped as a possibility for stardom in the Monroe mould, plays Bob's girlfriend, sharing his adventures and frustrations. He liked her. 'What a doll she was,' he observed later. 'The kind of girl you could take home to your mother — after you locked your father in the garage.'

The picture turned out to be a mediocre offering, despite Bob's insistence on re-writes and additions, on seeing the Hollywood preview, and a further $200,000 worth of re-takes. One of the re-stages was a 'Silver Bells' Christmas number from Jay Livingston and Ray Evans. Since Irving Berlin's 'White Christmas' had scooped the Christmas song market, the partners needed hard persuasion to attempt a Christmas number but, as their contract depended on it, they set to work. 'Silver Bells' became an enormous hit. Record sales topped 31 million, and 1.5 million copies of the sheet music were sold.

It was very much Hollywood practice to milk success, and after Hope's impact with the mini-spy series, first with Madeleine Carroll in *My Favourite Blonde* in 1942 and then with Dorothy Lamour in *My Favourite Brunette* in 1947, Paramount felt the time had come for a third running. This time they matched him with the Austrian-born beauty Hedy Lamarr in *My Favourite Spy.* The spy plot is a natural vehicle for the Hope brand of comedy and, just one or two slow-moving sequences apart, the picture more than meets the standards of the day.

Bob plays a dual role. As a second-rate burlesque comic, Peanuts White, his uncanny resemblance to super-spy Eric Augustine is spotted by government agents, and the unwitting Peanuts is assigned to impersonate the sleuth on a mission that takes him to Tangier. There he encounters Hedy Lamarr, who is also a spy, and the capers begin. It is a classic Hope comedy situation, with him playing the bumbling amateur caught up with professionals in a web of intrigue, and it makes for a sparklingly funny film.

Bob's comment: 'In *My Favourite Spy* I played two parts and both of them were Hedy Lamarr's lovers. How about that for overtime!'

By general consensus, one of the funniest sequences in the picture is when Bob, after converting Hedy Lamarr into a 'goody' and with her fouling up the enemy's carefully laid plans, makes his escape in a a wild chase aboard a fire engine. It could have been taken straight from an old Keystone Kops picture.

Because of the huge success of *The Paleface,* a sequel was inevitable. It came just four years after the original, with the release of *Son of Paleface* which again featured Jane Russell. Robert L. Welch again produced and Frank Tashlin, one of the two writers of the original screenplay, was joined by Robert Welch and Joseph Quillan to prepare a new script. It must have been a daunting prospect after the success of *The Paleface,* and it was to everyone's credit that the follow-up was every bit as funny.

This time round Bob plays the son of the late pioneer dentist, Painless Potter, a Harvard graduate called Junior, who sets out West to claim his inheritance. For good measure the picture features cowboy ace Roy Rogers, hot on the trail of a bandit, and, of course, his fabled horse Trigger. Miss Russell is 'Mike' and runs the Dirty Shame saloon, but she is also 'Torch', the bandit being pursued by Rogers.

The classical Western is outrageously spoofed in a hilarious presentation, and Bob pulls out all the stops in a continuation of self-denigration with the usual topping of false courage. He even funks fighting an old codger, when he realizes he is not as doddery as he thinks, but is flattened by him all the same; and in one side-splitting scene an electrifying kiss from the fulsome lips of the fulsome-breasted Miss Russell is enough to stiffen his whole body and set his spurs spinning wildly. The film has plenty of action and after a long chase Hope gets the girl — Roy Rogers settles for Trigger.

It is not surprising that the picture contained a reprise of the sensational hit song 'Buttons and Bows', but it also featured 'Four-legged Friend', the classic cowboy song forever associated with Rogers. This well-worked follow-up was impressively successful at the box office, stopping only marginally short of the original.

It would have been hard to find someone at this time who could top Bob Hope's impact in all media. In the early to mid-1950s he continued to enjoy success in pictures, on radio, in

In among the glory boys at a Reagan rally in 1970. With Bob are John Wayne, Ronald Reagan, Dean Martin and Frank Sinatra.

Time for a round at the Letchworth Garden City Golf Club with (left to right) Frank Bird, Ted Long and his publicity man Bobbie Bixler.

'This is Your Life' – with Lord Mountbatten and Eamonn Andrews after being lured to the television studios in the belief that he would be interviewed for a magazine programme.

Back in England in 1979 for his first variety season in Britain for twenty-six years. During his stay he celebrated his seventy-sixth birthday.

Bob makes a pilgrimage to the house of his birth in Eltham, south-east London and talks to the present owners, John and Flo Ching.

Relaxed and comfortable at the Symonds' Hertfordshire home.

On another pilgrimage to Hitchin the Hollywood star receives a
warm welcome from cousin Frank.

Mr and Mrs Bob Hope –
theirs is a model
marriage.

No one has a greater love
of golf than Bob Hope.
Here he is with a regular
golf partner, former US
President Gerald Ford.

With General James Joy, commander of the US Marines in
Lebanon, on Christmas morning, 1983, during a tour of the base in
Beirut.

Off the Lebanese coast aboard the *USS Guam* performing
with Brooke Shields.

Washington 1985 – the
82-year-old Hope plants
a kiss on a bust of himself
at the ceremony
dedicating the Bob Hope
USO Building.

'Bob-Hope's High-Flying
Birthday Extravaganza'
– at the Pope Air Force
Base in North Carolina
Bob celebrates his eighty-
fourth birthday with
Barbara Mandrell and
Brooke Shields.

Enjoying an English cuppa on a visit to Hitchin. Bob once said that
this was his favourite picture.

personal appearances, and on stage, and would go on to create his own individual niche in TV. At Paramount, however, the studio bosses hadn't yet abandoned the *Road* formula as a means of materializing queues at the box office. Before casting him with Mickey Rooney and Marilyn Maxwell in *Off Limits,* put out as *Military Policemen* in the UK — and incidentally ingeniously probing the possibilities of Hope and Rooney as a new comedy duo, they brought the comedy trio together again for *Road to Bali.*

It had been five years since the last epic, and there may well have been doubts about the wisdom of trying to revive a formula which had first touched the public's funny bone as long ago as twelve years before, but Paramount were more than willing to take the risk. So were Hope and Crosby, who each once more had a one-third stake in the picture. The choice of Lamour to make up the trio had often been questioned when *Road to Singapore* was being cast, for she had no reputation at the time as a comedienne; nor had she particularly generated one in the years since then. But for most people she somehow slotted perfectly into the Hope-Crosby style and Paramount once more brought her in to complete the team.

Reading into the situation from comments made by Dorothy later, it's not hard to believe that she hadn't completely forgiven Bob and Bing for not inviting her to share in the profits of the previous *Road* picture. This time round the situation was aggravated when the boys invited Dotty to cut an album of songs from the film. She told them that she didn't think it fair that she should get less from the record proceeds than they would receive, and nothing more was said. According to Dorothy, when Bing and Bob were not on the set one morning at the usual time, she felt hurt when she found out they had been recording some of the songs from the film, with Peggy Lee singing her part.

In *Road to Bali,* Bob and Bing are vaudeville performers in Australia who decide to get out of the country rapidly when they find themselves hotly pursued by a couple of marriage-minded girls. On a South Sea island they encounter Princess Lalah (Dorothy Lamour), who is looking for sunken treasure which rightly belongs to her and which is also being sought by villain Ken Arok, played by Murvyn Vye.

The location and the plot, such as it is, are merely there to provide the showcase typical of a *Road* comedy. The trio, in fact, tend to ignore the storyline — and who can blame them? There is much more to concentrate on as our heroes find themselves in all sorts of scrapes. Not only are comments from contemporary times blatantly punched into the script, but *Bali* features a succession of guest stars. Jane Russell, Dean Martin and Jerry Lewis, and Bing's brother Bob all materialize as the picture proceeds, but perhaps the funniest appearance is that of Academy Award winner Humphrey Bogart in a couple of sequences. Re-enacting the most dramatic scene from his award winning movie, *African Queen,* we see him dragging a boat through a swamp; later, in a mirage, when Crosby picks up Bogart's Oscar, Hope takes it from him, complaining: 'Give me that. You've already got one.'

Road fans gave a rapturous welcome to the sixth picture in the series, which retained a high standard. Bob's cowardice is played up with the style and panache which only he can create. The escapades follow fast, one after another, and at various times Bob and Bing encounter wild animals, a giant squid and even cannibals.

At one point Hope looks set to end up in the natives' cooking pot and, hilariously, seems to be considering whether that might not be preferable to submitting to the amorous advances of an extra-large, far-from-pretty native lady. At another point, trembling with terror, he announces to Bing: 'I can't stand torture. It hurts!'

The picture scores well in its own right, any criticism — and there was little of it — coming almost wholly from comparisons with previous adventures in the series. It was the first *Road* picture to be made in Technicolor and Paramount proclaimed through its billing that it was 'the Riotous Reunion you've been yellin' for'. The picture, incidentally, had started out as *Road to Hollywood,* but went through various re-writes and changes of approach before emerging as *Road to Bali.*

It was effectively the end of the *Road* series. Paramount tried to keep the idea going when they announced *The Road to the Moon* in the late 1950s, but it was never made, though it is said that some of the work done then was used for the ill-fated and ill-advised *Road to Hong Kong* which emerged years later.

The end of the *Road* pictures was also the end of an era for Hope, though materially there can have been few regrets. The seven pictures were once estimated to have earned a total of $50 million!

A comment which typified many a fan's fading memory of the series was expressed by Carlos Clarens some years later in *The Movie:* 'The *Roads* made Crosby, Hope and Lamour the screen's best-loved eternal triangle.'

8 The Greenway

To say merely that Bob Hope likes golf is similar to saying that he is in show business. Both understate the true position by prodigious margins. As an entertainer he gained immense stature and is without equal for the impact and success he achieved over so many years as a mass-media international star. As a golfer it would be hard to find another non-professional who enjoys the game more or who is more obsessive about golf.

It was way back in 1927, when he was twenty-four, that Bob had his first game of golf. It was on a public course in Cleveland. He reckoned he displayed such an appalling lack of natural aptitude that he packed it in there and then.

A vaudeville comedy act called the Diamond Brothers brought him back into the game. They were town-hopping the northern circuit in America together, doing matinees and evening performances, and Bob found himself with a lot of time on his hands in the morning. For a long time he used to sit in hotel lobbies watching the Diamond Brothers trundling through with their bags on the way to their regular sessions of golf. One day in 1930, in Seattle, they invited him to join them. He borrowed a set of clubs, seemed to perform much better this time and, most important, enjoyed the experience. In his own words: 'I got hooked on golf that day. I've been addicted to it ever since.'

It is useful that Dolores enjoys golf too. A few years ago, when Bob spent long months on tours entertaining the troops all over the world, at least they could get together on the golf course when he came home. In fact, Dolores has been a competent golfer most of her adult life. At the Lakeside Golf Club in North Hollywood she was the women's club runner-up five times. For a long time Bob kidded her about never becoming champion, but she did have the edge in Vienna of all places, when they played on a course constructed on the inside of a race track. In his book *Confessions of a Hooker*, written with Dwayne Netland, Bob explains: 'I played the course on Saturday and did pretty well. Dolores went out for her round the next day. When she had finished, one of the members stood up on the steps of the clubhouse and grandly announced: "Scores: Mr Bob Hope, 79; Mrs Bob Hope, 78." Dolores got a kick out of that.'

Bob has probably spent more time on the golf course than he has in his own luxurious homes, and he has played with equal pleasure with friends and casual acquaintances whose names mean nothing to the outside world, show business stars, politicians and presidents, and the top players from the pro circuit. His passionate love of the game has never diminished; and he plays better golf than ever he would admit — he enjoys carrying the self 'put-down' of the *Road* pictures.

Bob not only plays the game for pleasure. He blatantly uses it to uphold and extend his persona as the sharp-tongued comic who can see a joke in every situation. Those who play with him must first understand that they lay themselves bare to 'commercial exploitation', and nobody escapes the treatment, not even royalty and presidents. Indeed, least of all American presidents. Cracked Hope at one time when playing Gerald Ford, former US president and equally passionate about golf: 'There are forty-two golf courses in the Palm Springs area and nobody knows which one Ford is playing until after he hits his tee shot!'

He has played with John Kennedy, Lyndon Johnson, Ronald Reagan, Richard Nixon and Dwight Eisenhower, among others, and a string of pros and personalities including Bing, of course, Fred Astaire, Ed Sullivan, Arnold Palmer, Jackie Gleason, Billy Graham, Dinah Shore, Sammy Davis Jr, Dean Martin, Ruby Keeler, Paulette Goddard, Mickey Rooney, former boxing champion the late Joe Louis, Jack Benny, Ben Hogan, Jack Nicklaus, Sam Snead, Seve Ballesteros, Jim Garner, Telly Savalas and many, many others. Bob especially likes to mention one opponent, King Baudouin of Belgium. The royal game resulted from a party in Hollywood at which Bob and the King, then Prince Baudouin, were present. When the party broke up, the Prince told Hope to look him up if he was ever in Belgium. Two years later Bob took him up on the invitation. He was in London with his old friend Pardee Erdman recuperating from an eye operation and he phoned the royal palace from his suite at the Savoy. 'Would you tell the King that I'm in London and have golf clubs and will travel,' he instructed the royal equerry. Baudouin was delighted and arranged for a car to meet Bob and Erdman at the airport in Brussels the next day. Together with Jack Maurman, the Belgian Amateur champion, they played an enjoyable foursome on the royal course after having lunch with the King.

It would be hard to find a more extensive show business traveller than Bob Hope and almost always his golf clubs travelled with him. He reckons he must have played in a score or more countries, on famous and unknown courses, in the height of the summer and at Christmas. For Bob, golfing was for all seasons. A chink of a break in his punishing schedule was always enough for him to head for the nearest golf course. 'But isn't golf a wonderful game?' he'll say with obvious sincerity. In Alaska he has played at eleven o'clock at night. In Australia the weather has been so severe that he has been nearly blown off the course. In Korea, army engineers cleared the green of a foot of snow so that he could play golf.

Bob enjoys playing with the pros, but loves it as much when he and Dolores casually drive over to the nearby Lakeside course from their home in North Hollywood on Sunday afternoons. He admits to watching all the golf on television. He and Gerald Ford used to take part in the Ladies PGA pro-am until, quips Hope, 'Our wives discovered that provocative poster of Jan Stephenson, with the inscription, "Play a round with me".'

He has played a lot in Britain and in 1951 competed in the British Amateur Championship on the Royal Porthcawl course in Wales. He joked many years later about his handicap, claiming that, 'Dolores says there are days when I'm closer to shooting my weight than my age.' But in Britain in '51 he had been working very hard at his game and by the time he mailed his entry for the Porthcawl tournament his handicap was down to 4. The day was cold and rainy and Bob didn't do too well, being beaten in the first round of match play by a paint salesman from Yorkshire named Charlie Fox who wore glasses and smoked a pipe throughout the round. Bob later claimed it was all a huge plot engineered by Crosby — the pipe giving the game away — because it had been Bing who had suggested to Bob that he play at Porthcawl. (Crosby had played in the British Amateur the previous year at St Andrews and, although he lost his match, he enjoyed the experience and had a huge gallery.)

There was a gallery of over a thousand for Hope and Charlie Fox's game. After it was all over, Bob invited quite a crowd back to his 'hotel', which was in fact St Donat's Castle, six miles from Cardiff, where he was staying by courtesy of Dick Berlin, who worked for William Randolph Hearst, the American newspaper magnate, who died that same year. The place was massive, and Hope reckoned it had thirty-six suites and he was the only person staying there at the time. But by all accounts, the post-golf party was quite an experience.

All told, European courses are not his particular favourites. He says that Scottish golf is great, 'but St Andrews and Gleneagles have traps where you get in and you're never heard from again.' His most enjoyable golf is played at Palm Springs, at several desert clubs, including Canyon and Eldorado. They are both within about fifteen minutes' travelling time from the magnificent 25,000 square feet of 'Space Age' home which Bob and Dolores had built in 1980.

Bob has always taken his golf seriously, but was never the sort who lets a poor shot or a bad game put him down. Much of his enjoyment stems from being out in the fresh air, the exercise, the companionship surrounding golf, and the sheer beauty of some of the famous courses. He gives Alex Morrison credit for improving his game in the early days in New York, when he used to attend Morrison's driving range on 59th Street, and the seven years he lived in New York gave him ample opportunity to get out to all the local clubs.

It was at Alex Morrison's driving range that Bob and Bing hit golf balls together for the first time. Soon Crosby was in Hollywood making a big name for himself in pictures — and playing regularly as a prominent member of the Lakeside Club. When Bob and Dolores followed him to Hollywood some five years later, Bob's game had improved significantly. A lot of his fondest memories of Bing are taken from the many rounds of golf they played together around the world. And even Bob had to admit: 'Bing was always a little better than I was.' Bing was probably even more consumed by the game than Bob and would often be up by six in the morning playing a few holes. As they got older, Bob eased back and would only play nine holes. Bing, though warned only a short time before by a doctor in the UK to take life easier and to play only nine holes because of his heart, had just finished eighteen holes when he collapsed and died from a heart attack on his way back to the clubhouse at La Moraleja Club, near Madrid in Spain. It was a body blow for Hope, who had shared so much over so many years, with Bing.

In the early 1940s, before America entered the war, Bob and Bing played exhibition matches for the War Relief Fund and after Pearl Harbor this developed into a major series of golf matches tied in to broadcasts from military bases. It brought in millions of dollars in war bonds.

Bob Hope has probably played golf with more professionals and more often than any other amateur golfer, and he admits you can learn a lot from the experience. You get the feeling that probably Arnold Palmer would be his all-time favourite. Bob followed his career systematically from the time he first saw him play in the mid-1950s. Someone told Bob at that time that Palmer was destined to become a great champion, and he had so much power that Bob wasn't at all surprised to hear the prediction. A decade later the two were firm friends, Bob having had him as a guest on his television show and then enticing him to Kenya for a novelty spot in his film *Call Me Bwana,* in which he starred with Anita Ekberg. Bob not only admired Palmer's undoubted skill on a golf course, with all those tournament victories and honours to prove it, but the charismatic nature of the man appealed enormously to his sense of showmanship.

Non-golfing film buffs are likely to know Bob the golfer more from the massive publicity he has gained from his games with his country's leading politicians, even presidents, than from his contact with the pros, the pro-am competitions aside. Indeed, cynics might well argue that the fostering of such liaisons, and the enormous worldwide publicity which has resulted from them, has all been a careful and skilful plot hatched by the media-minded Hope. It is hardly likely to be the case. Even without golf, Bob's talents were destined to take him into high places, there to rub shoulders naturally with the top people in all walks of life. And since many of them shared his enthusiasm for the game, what more natural than that they should play golf together? That the personalities involved should become a reservoir for more jokes was inevitable, given his brand of humour.

In any event, this certainly was not the case with 'Ike', wartime General Eisenhower who became US President, for according to Bob it was Ike who first brought up the subject of golf at their very first meeting. In fact, Bob has reported, his first words on their meeting were: 'How's your golf?' That was in 1943, during Bob's series of shows for US servicemen in North Africa. He played countless times with Ike after that.

No president's golfing ability was made more fun of by Bob than Gerald Ford's. 'He made golf a contact sport,' Bob quipped, and admits to getting a lot of mileage from his Gerry Ford jokes. One of the best and most reported perhaps is this: 'You all know Gerry Ford — the most dangerous driver since Ben Hur.' And: 'You must remember to be on the alert when you're playing with Gerry Ford. The only safe place to be is right behind him.' The two played a lot of golf together, and Ford was never troubled by Bob's incessant joking. The two remained excellent friends even after Ford left the White House and had little public impact. When Bob and Dolores stayed at their Palm Springs home, an early priority was always a game of golf with Ford, who lived nearby, at one of Bob's favourite courses, at perhaps $5 a hole.

In the 1980s pro-am celebrity golf brought the game into much stronger focus for a much enlarged public audience. The American show business tradition in golf began largely with Bing Crosby, who established his own tournament. Hope followed Crosby's example, organizing and inspiring a major event in which amateurs — for a sizeable fee which goes to charity — play alongside their favourite professionals.

This novel concept was transferred with suitable fanfare and outstanding success to Britain in September 1980 when the Bob Hope British Classic took place at the RAC Country Club in Epsom. The phenomenon of such an event is that it is the amateurs whom the public flock to see, not the pros. Such showbiz personalities as Sean Connery, Telly Savalas, Henry Cooper, Dickie Henderson, Eric Sykes, Bruce Forsyth, Jimmy Tarbuck, Ian Botham, Billy Wright and of course Bob Hope himself pulled in enormous crowds. Over 55,000 attended the four-day match and more than sixteen million watched it on television. Advance ticket sales were more than for any other tournament of its kind in the country, except for the traditional British Open, and brought in more than £25,000. The whole affair, with justification, was billed as the golfing showpiece of the season.

Said *Golf Illustrated* at the time: 'It is the first time that golf in Britain has staged a major 72-hole tournament where professionals and amateurs play as partners — for the professionals there is £100,000 in prize money on offer, and for the amateurs competing, the thrill of playing alongside a different top pro on each of the four days of the tournament.'

Bob has explained that this event had its origins in a visit he made to Britain in 1961 to make *Road to Hong Kong* with Bing, Joan Collins and Dorothy Lamour. He was visited on the set one day by former British Foreign Secretary Herbert Morrison, who suggested Bob visit Blackheath, to see 'your golf course' and, intrigued, he went along with the idea. Morrison was referring to the Roman battleground site on which Blackheath was built, only a stone's throw away from Bob's birthplace at Eltham. Their visit together gave him the idea of providing something for the people of his birth town to enjoy, and he decided it would be appropriate if he were to have a theatre built there.

Many busy years elapsed, but when the late Dickie Henderson in particular began urging him to get involved personally with an event to be called the Bob Hope British Classic, he realized that it could be an ideal way of raising funds for the theatre.

All the attendant razzmatazz was thrown into the event to exploit possible commercial opportunity to swell the financial take, with the Stars Organization for Spastics and the Bob Hope Theatre of the Arts Foundation in Eltham standing to benefit. Bob flung himself into the venture with his customary zeal and enthusiasm. With virtually everything hinging on the pulling power of the Bob Hope name, the three major sponsors were given the attractive concessions at the tournament, including their own sponsorship day on television, hospitality facilities and tickets for the gala dinner at the Grosvenor House Hotel, at which guests would be entertained by Hope and his friends.

The whole tournament was sensational and made such an impact that the event returned the following year, to be held at Moor Park in Hertfordshire, where it returned yet again in 1982.

'In 1982 the tournament really caught on, with celebrity attractions like Gerald Ford, Jim Garner, Telly Savalas, Seve Ballesteros and Sam Snead in attendance. And the theatre in Eltham was built,' Bob said.

This outstanding tournament was back in Britain once more in 1983, but even before that there were rumblings that all was not well. In October 1982 entertainer Dickie Henderson, who had thought up the idea of the Classic for Britain with business-man John Spurling, was finding it necessary to defend the event in the pages of *Golf Illustrated* against what he called 'a campaign of innuendo'. This was in response to certain national newspaper claims that the Charity Commissioners were looking into the organizing companies' books. John Spurling reportedly added: 'For the first two years the tournament lost money. This year [1982] it is in the black. The losses in the last couple of years amounted to around £430,000. We will not only cover that but expect to be £120,000 in the black.'

Meantime, Bob appeared unperturbed, in spite of someone phoning to tell him that the money set aside for charity from the first and second British Classics — around £130,000 — had come from loans. 'Wonderful,' he said. 'The main thing is that charity got its money — that's the bottom line. That's why we're all over here.' He also said he considered it marvellous that the company was in the black after only three years when there were tournaments in America still losing money after ten years. When the news broke that the Bob Hope British Classic, despite its vir-tuous ideals, public impact and exciting image, had crashed out of existence with debts estimated at more than half a million pounds, leaving more than seventy dejected creditors, not everyone was taken completely by surprise. As early as December 1982 the editor of the British publication *Golf World* had run a major three-page feature in which John Spurling repeated what Dickie Henderson had said two months before about a 'campaign of trial and innuendo' concerning the event. In an exclusive interview with Spurling conducted by *Golf World* editor Peter Haslam, it was reported that most of that publicity had arisen from the relationship between income and charity benefit. From an overall income of millions of pounds from the first two years, according to the article less than £150,000 had eventually found its way to charities.

The spirited and gala atmosphere which had surrounded the Bob Hope British Classic when it started out was sadly extinguished amid a welter of confusing and often conflicting evidence concerning expensive flight and hotel bills, extravagant entertaining, high running costs, payment to celebrities for appearing in event-related cabarets, and appearance money for the pros to persuade them to take part in the tournament. While Spurling denied many or even all of these allegations, the depressing consequence was that Bob Hope's dream for charity was shattered and the event collapsed.

While it is important to be clear that nobody doubted Bob Hope's integrity, there is no doubt that he carried some of the mud from the demise of the ill-fated tournament around with him for quite some time, certainly in Britain. In February 1984, *Golf Monthly* editor Malcolm Campbell wrote: 'It emerges that there was very little amateur, or even charitable, spirit about his [Hope's] connection with the Bob Hope British Classic.' And in the end there was the spectacle of public disagreement between John Spurling and Bob over the extent of fees and expenses the latter had received over the last two years of the event.

Looking back on the débâcle in August 1986, *Golf World* editor Peter Haslam told me: 'When the Bob Hope Classic failed, it went out in a blaze of bad publicity. Bob Hope himself must take some of the blame for the debts which accrued. Quite a number of British firms were in serious financial difficulty because they were not paid their due money by the Classic.'

Haslam's personal view is that Bob might have considered dipping into his own vast coffers to rescue an event which, after all, was built around him and carried his name. He added: 'Sadly, he did not and I have a feeling that he might now regret not having done so.' Certainly charities did benefit from the Classic, which is about the only consolation which can be claimed from the wreckage of an altogether miserable experience.

For someone like Bob, who loves golf so much and has given prodigiously of his personal time, effort and talent to the cause of charity over so many years, the Bob Hope British Classic must still occasionally materialize as a nightmare, but overall he has emerged remarkably unscathed, both personally and in reputation. His fans have long since forgotten, and the general public have long since forgiven him. Hope jokes about everything, but it's hard to find a gag of his about the British Classic.

A much happier experience came from a source nearer home. The Bob Hope Desert Classic had its origins in the Palm Springs Golf Classic which began in 1960. When, a few years later, Bob was asked to put his name to it, he declined because of lack of time. In 1965, under further pressure to find a sponsor for the event, he approached Chrysler and they agreed to back it, providing it became the Bob Hope Desert Classic. In the early years he used to play through the whole tournament, but later he eased back, though still involved himself considerably in the event.

It was Bob's influence and involvement that roped in all the top names which made it such a rich and successful social occasion as well as a golfing event. Within just a year or two of its relaunch under his name, it had become probably the biggest golf tournament in the world, with over 120 professionals and almost 390 amateurs playing for a total purse of $110,000. Charity was the declared beneficiary, with seventy per cent of the cash going to the Eisenhower Medical Centre (some $10 million eventually being raised for its construction) and the remainder to many charities in the Palm Springs region.

Work was started on the centre in 1969, on eighty acres of land which Bob owned and gave over, and Dolores was president of the centre for seven years before becoming chairman. A dedication ceremony was held in 1971. Eisenhower by that time had died, but the former President's wife, Mamie, attended the ceremony along with President Nixon, Vice-President Agnew and the then governor of California, Ronald Reagan.

Unlike the Bob Hope British Classic, the Bob Hope Desert Classic is an experience he is well able to joke about and often does. 'My only regret is that they don't have an intensive care unit in the Eisenhower Medical Centre for my golf game,' is a typical gag.

9 A Turn in the Road

After *Road to Bali* in 1952 only once did Bob, Bing and Dotty appear together again in a picture. That was the disappointing, ill-advised *Road to Hong Kong* in 1962.

The break brought mixed fortunes for the famous trio. It virtually signalled the end of Lamour's screen career. In 1952 she was approaching thirty-six, no longer the natural choice to fit into a sarong, and with good roles hard to find, she found consolation in moving onto the nightclub circuit. Between the two *Roads* she did not appear even once on the silver screen, and she was featured in only two more pictures before her movie career ended in the mid-1960s.

Crosby fared better. Among the few more movies he made were the fabulously successful *White Christmas* in 1954 and *High Society* in 1956.

Of the three, Bob Hope's film career was by far the most extensive. Between *Bali* and *Hong Kong* he appeared in six more films at Paramount, two for Metro-Goldwyn-Mayer and four for United Artists, including *Road to Hong Kong*. Between 1962 and the effective end of his movie career in 1972, he did one more picture for MGM, two for Warner Brothers, one for Cinerama and five for United Artists. Collectively they were a poor lot, bearing no comparison with his earlier offerings, but he managed to maintain one tradition, appearing with some of the most glamorous co-stars in the business. Among those with whom he appeared in the second half of the 1950s and the 1960s were Eva Marie Saint, Vera Miles, Alexis Smith, Anita Ekberg, Rhonda Fleming, Lana Turner, Tuesday Weld, Elke Sommer and Gina Lollobrigida.

After *Bali,* Bob had two films released in 1953, one in 1954 and one more in 1955. Of the 1953 movies, *Off Limits,* in which he co-starred with Mickey Rooney and singing blonde Marilyn Maxwell, was the better choice. Hope and Rooney worked well together on the comedy routines. Released in the UK as *Military Policemen,* the film was directed by George Marshall with Harry Tugend producing and told the story of the boxing manager who joins the army to be near his conscripted protégé only to find that once he is well and truly in the army, the boxer is rejected for service. Hope plays the manager and Rooney the boxer he discovers. Hope falls in love with the boxer's aunt, played by Marilyn Maxwell. Theoretically, the picture had a more substantial plot than many of his earlier films, but somehow the script seemed weaker and, although there were some funny sequences, it created little impact.

Here Come the Girls (1953) and *Casanova's Big Night* (1954) did little to reflate his flagging career. In the former he appears with Tony Martin, Arlene Dahl and Rosemary Clooney — all distinguished performers with solid reputations, but the plot is tiresome, though the film returned reasonable business at the box office. *Casanova's Big Night* was an attempt to capitalize on his 1946 success, *Monsieur Beaucaire,* casting him as a tailor's assistant who masquerades as Casanova so he can test the faithfulness of a nobleman's fiancée. Joan Fontaine stars with him in a picture in which he does what he can with a story which loses pace in parts and struggles unsuccessfully to keep up interest. The slapstick fight duel between Bob, as a dowager, and Basil Rathbone provides the best sequence in a film which also included former boxing champion Primo Carnera, Hugh Marlowe, John Carradine, Lon Chaney Jr and Raymond Burr. Bob still had a healthy reputation at the box office, however, and the film made $3 million.

His offering in 1955 was *The Seven Little Foys,* which was a 'biopic' of vaudevillian Eddie Foy. Foy had been an interesting character. After the death of his wife he was faced with bringing up his seven children by himself and hit on the idea of reorganizing his vaudeville act to include them in his performance. The result was the most famous family act ever to appear in vaudeville. A couple of Hope's gag-writers had thought up the idea of a picture based on Foy's life, and Hope responded enthusiastically because it would give him his first opportunity to play a real-life character. 'I saw *The Seven Little Foys* as a real challenge,' he said afterwards. He was so intent on doing it that his razor-sharp intuition for the commercial aspect of his work was allowed to lapse, for the package the two writers

— Jack Rose and Mel Shavelson — put up meant that he would receive no salary, but would have an equal share with them in any profits which the picture might make. He agreed and the package was then sold to Paramount.

Said Bob in *The Road to Hollywood:* 'I had some pretty heavy dramatics to perform. I wanted to capture Eddie Foy as well as I could, and I studied everything I could find about his life, including some silent movies he had made. I received a great deal of help from the Foys themselves, especially Bryan, Eddie Jr and Charley, who was the technical adviser on the picture.'

James Cagney guested on the picture, playing the part of George M. Cohan, the famous patriotic songwriter, as a tribute to the help and support he had received from Eddie Foy and his wife when he was struggling to make his way in show business. (In the 1940s Cagney had won the best actor award for his portrayal of Cohan in the successful biopic *Yankee Doodle Dandy.*) One of the most memorable features of the film was his tap duet with Bob. Before gaining fame in his legendary gangster roles in the 1930s, Cagney had been a talented dancer, and for this guest appearance sequence both he and Bob worked hard on the number. This particular clip still comes over very well, though Cagney is seen as having the more natural style and stature as a dancing man. Bob, let it be said, performed commendably, however, not only in the dance number, but as a straight actor in a film which at times demanded a lot from the world's top comedian.

One assessment of the picture said it was so cliché-ridden that fewer fans than usual were amused, while another said that, 'While being in no danger of winning any Oscars, it had a less phoney ring than the average show business biopic, and gave a lot of ticket buyers a good time.' Whatever the truth, Bob himself seemed reasonably happy all round at the outcome, considering the result well worth all the effort. 'Not only did it place me in another category as a performer, but it also made a mint of money — and Hope Enterprises owned forty-four per cent of the take,' he wrote.

Two more Hope films were released in 1956 and another in 1957, but his tenure at Paramount was now rapidly approaching its end. *That Certain Feeling* was made at Paramount. It started out with little promise and in the end was seen as a distinctly meritorious production. On the other hand, *The Iron Petticoat,* which was shot very soon after, was filled with a promise which was never fulfilled, and it soon disappeared in a public parade of acrimonious comment.

Norman Panama and Melvin Frank were once more the basis of the success of *That Certain Feeling*. Their professional scripting, based on the Jean Kerr-Eleanor Brooke Broadway comedy success *King of Hearts* was immaculate and Panama's direction superb. Hope plays Francis X. Dignan, a talented cartoonist whose marriage to Dunreath (Eva Marie Saint) fails. Dunreath works for comic-strip artist Larry Larkin (George Sanders) as his secretary. When Larry hires Francis as his assistant, Francis tries to halt the developing love-relationship and prospective marriage of his former wife and Larkin. Three popular songs were all featured in the film — 'Hit the Road to Dreamland', 'Zing! went the Strings of My Heart', and of course 'That Certain Feeling'. Bob turned in an extremely adept performance, one assessment claiming it to be without doubt his most sophisticated motion picture to that time. The film also benefited from the additional authority of Eva Marie Saint, who had not long before won an Academy Award for her performance opposite Marlon Brando in *On the Waterfront*.

The Iron Petticoat was originally intended as a *Ninotchka*-type story featuring Hollywood legends Katherine Hepburn and Cary Grant, to be shot in Britain under the MGM banner, but when Grant wasn't available, someone suggested that Bob take over the part, mainly on the strength of his performance in *The Seven Little Foys*. He was delighted and even a little intimidated by Hepburn's reputation, but he considered it a great privilege and opportunity, and looked forward to doing a film in Britain for the first time, and to being able to visit his birthplace and look up relatives.

Once in Britain he was shocked by his first sight of the Ben Hecht script. He claimed it wasn't finished, but Hecht didn't seem unduly perturbed. In an effort to get the story completed, Bob injected some ideas and got a couple of his scriptwriters working on the closing scenes, but neither Hecht nor Hepburn were reportedly very pleased about the way the story was developing, though, according to Bob, Ben didn't seem able to contribute much himself. The picture had been known earlier as *Not For Money*, but after Bob's writers became increasingly involved in doctoring the script, it was renamed *The Iron Petticoat*, Hecht departed and later publicly disassociated himself from the venture with full-page Hollywood trade-paper ads in which he said he had removed his name as author and that Hepburn would also have extracted herself from the project had it been a practical possibility. Bob countered in the same way, stating that the picture was better for Hecht's departure. That is very doubtful, but the sad fact is that the picture was poor and perhaps misguided in retrospect, and was soon withdrawn.

According to Bob, he had to spend a long time persuading Paramount that he could be convincing in the role of the famous New York City Mayor of the 1920s, Jimmy Walker, hero of *Beau James*. Walker was full of charisma, seldom out of the headlines for one reason or another, a charmer, a rogue, a public figure occupying a position of power and drama in New York's most vivid, spectacular and exciting days.

Jack Rose and Melville Shavelson based their script on Gene Fowler's book, and it was they who persuaded Bob to try this straight dramatic and by no means easy role.

Mayor Walker's political career is under threat when, as a Catholic with a wife (Alexis Smith), he falls in love with an actress, Betty Compton, played by Vera Miles. The tension and drama build as Walker, whose enforced corruption and infidelity could perhaps have been probed with greater candour in the film, is eventually hounded out of the city he loves, his flamboyance deflated, a miserable and broken man. Bob's overall performance is admirable and convincing, and in one or two sequences he manages an impressive portrayal which clears out totally from the mind of the cinema-goer any cobwebs which might have remained from his days as the cinema's biggest joker. The picture also scores through its song standards, including 'Sidewalks of New York', 'Will You Love Me in December as You Do in May?', and 'Manhattan'.

Beau James was a milestone in the cinema career of Bob Hope. He had spent twenty years at Paramount, where he had made thirty-six full-length feature films. But the Paramount connection was now at an end and although he was to spend another fifteen years making pictures, not once again did he make a film for that studio. The reason for the switch was based on his becoming an independent film-maker through his company, Hope Enterprises, coupled with changes in the picture industry which provided him with greater scope only through a move to United Artists. There had been a growing trend for the major studios to accept the work of independent companies and their productions, and indeed by 1958 the proportion of Hollywood movies being made by independents would rise to sixty-five per cent. For a variety of reasons United Artists were able to accept these changes more enthusiastically than some of the larger studios, and it was Otto Preminger who said that: 'Only United Artists has a system of true independent production. They recognize that the independent has his own personality.' Bob thus switched to a studio which by the end of the 1950s had about fifty independent producers on their books, including Gregory Peck, John Wayne, Frank Sinatra and Robert Mitchum as well as Bob Hope.

Sadly, independence did not yield better movies in Bob's case, for, with one or two exceptions, from this point his material became weaker, his performances less effective in terms of critical acclaim and, in general, in box-office appeal too. Why did he bother to make movies at all? He wasn't in need of the cash. He didn't need them to keep him occupied, for he had a full schedule with radio and personal appearances, and his impact on television was rapidly gaining momentum. Maybe it was because, as he said, you don't know whether a movie is good or bad until after you've made it.

Paris Holiday was the first of his offerings to be made under the United Artists banner. He wrote the story, produced it and starred in it with Fernandel, France's top comedian. The talented combination, with Swedish beauty Anita Ekberg as a bonus, should have produced more laughs and a more captivating presentation, but the outcome was disappointing. Production costs went heavily into the red — according to Bob, as much as $1 million. Even he admitted he hadn't made much of a job of his first stab at picture production. His next picture was better: at least he produced it without exceeding the budget. *Alias Jesse James* took him out west as an insurance salesman who sells a policy to outlaw Jesse James and ends up having to protect his client. The situations are predictable, some with saloon singer Coral Lee Collins, and James's girlfriend (played by Rhonda Fleming), and while there are a number of sequences which point to Bob at his best, on the whole he had been much funnier.

Norman Panama and Melvin Frank hadn't written a screenplay for him since *That Certain Feeling,* released in 1956. It might not have been the best thing he had ever done, but it was a good picture, well presented and professionally handled, infinitely better than anything he had done since, so when they came up with an idea for him to co-star with Lucille Ball in *The Facts of Life* he was more than willing to listen, even though he was cast in a non-typical Hope part.

Originally patterned along the lines of the successful British movie *Brief Encounter, The Facts of Life* set out to explore the adultery theme American-style, and Panama and Frank originally wrote it with Olivia de Havilland and William Holden in mind. There were doubts about the script, and while Panama and Frank were working to get it right, a picture along similar lines came out featuring Kim Novak and Kirk Douglas. They were about to put their script away when Frank had the idea that, with the somewhat different slant which Hope and Ball could give to the picture, it might yet be saved.

It was an amiable film about a married man and married woman, each unhappy with their partners, who decide to have an affair, but the difficulties of trying to arrange clandestine meetings, coupled with their wholesome reputation among friends and families, are just too much and they decide to end the relationship. Both Hope and Ball did a worthy job in submerging their own characters and personalities, not an easy discipline for either, but the film pleased their respective fans, gained a fair measure of critical success, and registered well at the box office.

Bob next appeared with Lana Turner in MGM's *Bachelor in Paradise*, a rather tame domestic comedy which had little impact on those involved in making it or on the public who were supposed to enjoy it, so it is hardly surprising that he was again receptive when Panama and Frank once more came to the rescue with what seemed like an inspirational idea — another *Road* picture. Why not indeed? It had been nearly ten years since the last *Road* movie had been released and with Bob, Bing and Dotty all available, the power of nostalgia alone provided all the motivation necessary to get the project off the ground. There was also optimism that, with luck, the picture could well hit the jackpot commercially.

In the wake of such anticipation, its relative failure and the shameful treatment of Lamour left a sad and disappointing legacy. It never remotely challenged the pitch and spirit of the earlier *Roads* and was soon dismissed as an unfortunate and unworthy end to the series.

Dotty had her doubts about her part in the film from an early stage. Rumours about another *Road* picture, to be made in London, had been sneaking into the showbiz columns, and she was particularly hurt when she read that Sophia Loren and Gina Lollobrigida were among those being tipped to take her part, because she had heard nothing officially about the film. She had been left to find out for herself by the time Norman Panama dropped off a copy of the script for her to look over, together with a new song which Sammy Cahn had written for her to handle in the picture.

She was incensed by the 'giveaway' part she had been given — '... a couple of pages of dialogue that an extra could have handled,' she said later. She claimed she had already made it clear that in any new *Road* picture she would never tolerate any minimizing of her role, feeling it would be humiliating since all three of them had starred in the earlier pictures. She could understand if a bigger box-office draw would be wanted to play opposite Bob and Bing, leaving her out of the picture altogether. After all, she had been in semi-retirement for some four years and was now forty-six — though still several years younger than both Bob and Bing.

Dotty flatly turned down the part, agreeing to look at it again only when or if it had been built up. For a while there was silence. Then Mel Frank tried to persuade her to change her mind, claiming that it was much too late to alter the script. For a time she stuck it out as Mel called her repeatedly, urging her to have a change of heart. It didn't soften her attitude to discover that they wanted her so badly because she had been committed, along with Hope and Crosby, in the contract deal struck with United Artists, who were to distribute the picture. Dotty said later that, when the picture seemed to be in jeopardy, and for old times' sake, she relented and came to their rescue — 'but at a price, with a few zeros added to it.'

Bob tended to avoid the issue afterwards when writing about *Road to Hong Kong,* preferring to concentrate on the good time he and Crosby had during the making of the film in Britain, sharing with their respective families the luxurious Cranbourne Court at a rent of $1,000 a week and sneaking off at every opportunity to play golf at nearby courses. But it seemed that Bob was never in favour of replacing Lamour and was unhappy with the treatment she received. One source reckoned that it was he who finally

persuaded her to join the film, and certainly the relationship between the two didn't appear to have suffered, for she willingly
agreed to travel to Hollywood from her home in Baltimore to
help Bob promote the picture on his television show. When she
offered to make a similar appearance for Bing, who was also
doing a television special to promote the movie, she said he made
some excuse about its being too late to write her into the script.
Said Dotty in her autobiography: 'When I saw his special,
however, I was really shocked to see them using large blow-ups
of me, and they kept talking about me all through the show. I
couldn't understand what had happened to Bing. Sometimes, as
in England, he could be as sweet as ever, and then an aloofness
would set in that had never been there before.'

The news of Lamour's shabby treatment brought a surge of
sympathy, and when the unit arrived in Britain for the shooting
she was besieged by reporters and photographers, which gave
the picture enormous publicity. It amused her to discover that,
although Joan Collins was the new star, all the headlines
proclaimed that Bob, Bing and Dotty were together again on a
new *Road* adventure. There was newspaper talk of a feud
developing between Lamour and Collins, a fairly obvious angle
for journalists to play up, but according to Dotty this was never
true. Her part was exceptionally brief and, in spite of all the
pressure and publicity, was never built up. But, according to
Dotty, there was still plenty of fun between the famous three
once shooting began.

'Personally, I was able to forget the hassles and began to enjoy
working with those two guys again,' she said. 'When Bob made
some silly remark about the old gal in the sarong, I retorted: "If
you're not careful I'll hit you over the head with some of my fan
mail".'

Despite appearances, Bing didn't have everything his own
way in *Road to Hong Kong.* According to stories circulating at the
time he had really wanted Brigitte Bardot instead of Dorothy to
provide the love interest, but in the end had to settle for Joan
Collins. The entire situation seemed rather hard on Collins, who
in a sense was the innocent party in all this, but her inclusion
certainly wasn't enough to lift the picture out of its general lack
of zest and spirit. The key element which had stamped the earlier
Roads with a special kind of magic was absent in this final fling.
'Teamwork' was a big song from the film and went on to become

something of a minor classic of its kind, but some of the better moments came not from the three stars' teamwork but from a string of guest appearances by the likes of Frank Sinatra, Dean Martin, David Niven, Zsa Zsa Gabor, dear old Jerry Colonna and Peter Sellers, whose Indian doctor characterization was extremely funny.

The overall verdict was that this was by far the poorest of the *Road* films, with Bob and Bing trying vainly to recapture a particular spark which perhaps time itself had extinguished. If any consolation was necessary, then perhaps *Time* magazine offered it when it reported that the seven *Road* films were said to have earned a total of $50 million worldwide. The take has surely gone up since then.

After *Road to Hong Kong* Bob spent another ten years making nine more movies before dropping the curtain on his screen career. Even collectively they amounted to little. His offerings in 1963 were *Critic's Choice,* made at Warner Brothers, with Lucille Ball and Marilyn Maxwell, and *Call Me Bwana,* released through United Artists, with Anita Ekberg. In 1964 *A Global Affair,* distributed through MGM, had him appearing with Lilo Pulver, Michèle Mercier, Elga Andersen and Yvonne de Carlo in a story about an abandoned baby discovered in the United Nations building, and this was followed a year later by *I'll Take Sweden* with Tuesday Weld, Frankie Avalon and former British beauty queen Rosemarie Frankland.

In 1966 *Boy, Did I Get a Wrong Number* brought him together for the first time with zany comedienne Phyllis Diller. In a minor flurry which hinted at a last-ditch attempt to squeeze a mini-series out of what was left of his flagging film career, Diller appeared with him in his next two pictures — *Eight on the Lam* (*Eight on the Run* in Great Britain), and *The Private Navy of Sergeant O'Farrell,* released in 1967 and 1968 respectively. The former did well in the United States, but received scant attention in Britain, and Bob's two grandchildren, Avis and Robert Hope, appeared in it. In the latter, there is a fleeting reminder of better days on the *Road* as the action takes place on a South Pacific island, but Phyllis Diller as a dizzy nurse, a Japanese soldier called Mako and the delectable Gina Lollobrigida as a former sweetheart fail to raise much interest or appeal. *How to Commit Marriage,* in which Hope appeared with Jane Wyman and Jackie Gleason, was released in 1971 and then, in October the following year, there was *Cancel My Reservation* with Eva Marie Saint, Ralph Bellamy, Forrest Tucker and Keenan Wynn. The film was a disappointment, and perhaps by then even Bob had realized that his movie career was virtually at an end.

Not that it bothered him, by all accounts. In a sense he might well have realized that he had been living on borrowed time for a few years, and in any event the end of Bob Hope the film star was by no means a financial tragedy. The furious pace of his life, for which by now he had become famous, hadn't slackened. Indeed, with the fast-developing impact of television, the demands on his time had increased rather than diminished. At first he wasn't at ease with the new medium, but his growing mastery over it and the way he adapted his instinctive approach made him a television superstar, acclaimed by vast audiences in the United States.

Bob had begun to take a serious interest in television in the 1950s, though his occasional contact with the new medium had been made much earlier. A guest appearance on the Ed Sullivan Show *Toast of the Town* in 1949 sharpened his appetite, but the film studio discouraged him. His movie career with Paramount was then in full flood and they were afraid that, if he appeared on television too frequently, over-exposure might blunt his big-screen appeal. Such was his impact, however, that when he did take the plunge with his first NBC network single sponsored by Frigidaire in April 1950, he was paid the enormous sum of $40,000, said to be four times the previous top fee for a television one-off show. From that moment Bob Hope was finally anchored to the television scene, but he played it on his terms and as a result outlasted all his contemporaries in terms of television life and popularity. From the start he refused to submit to the regular chore of a weekly series, a policy probably forced on him by the incredibly heavy demands made on his time by radio, personal appearances, movies and tours overseas. Viewers didn't tire of him, and under that first contract he did three more shows for Frigidaire. When he did appear, it was always something of an occasion, though his first show was given a tepid reception by the critics, who, though they looked with somewhat more favour on his television style and performance than on his new films, never made him one of their favourites, though his appeal among viewers was such that he could almost pick and choose his sponsors. A Bob Hope television special was guaranteed to be somewhere near the top in the ratings.

Bob took a little while to master the new technique. He had been used to working at a fast rate on radio, a style which resulted from his service shows, where too much finesse on timing was lost on audiences who wanted the gags, and as many of them as they could get in the time Bob was on stage. Radio is also a quicker medium than television. On television, there is much closer contact with an audience. It is more intimate than radio. Audiences are taking in the visual element as well as the sound, and it is important to ease the pace. Bob said later that he found the secret of successful television performance was being relaxed, casual and easy. He learned to slow down for television, especially with his monologues. 'It's as much the way you say it as what you say on television,' he said.

Bob's early attitude towards television had been cool. Rumour has it that, when first approached for the lucrative Frigidaire single, he was extremely unenthusiastic, adding that he was busy enough without television and didn't know much about it anyway. 'You can't pay me enough,' was his alleged answer when asked what it would take to change his mind. Then, still being pressed, he responded: 'Fifty thousand.' He considered it a figure big enough to end the discussion. The final agreed package brought him a total of $150,000 for four additional shows, plus a compromise $40,000 for his début feature performance on television.

In the meantime, showing that he always considered himself an all-round performer, not tied to a particular medium, Bob made a swift and profitable return to vaudeville by signing a contract for $50,000 a week to appear at New York's Paramount Theatre, hiring Jane Russell and the Les Brown Band to share the stage with him.

Having a cluster of stars around him has always been a Hope trademark, and he carried it forward into television. His first show for Frigidaire brought on guest stars Douglas Fairbanks Jr, Dinah Shore and Beatrice Lillie; his second featured big-name singers Frank Sinatra and Peggy Lee. He had been unusually nervous before his first major television show and at the end was disappointed at his performance. In the second show, he responded to the cool attitude of the critics with typical flamboyance, making direct reference to their opinions and gagging about the money he was receiving. 'I want to thank the thousands who wrote letters about the first show ... and the three who mailed them,' he joked. Bob Hope on television held out so much promise, however, that when he fell out with Lever Brothers and his radio contract was ended, he was quickly signed to an exclusive long-term contract with NBC for both radio and television which together would net him close to a million dollars a year.

Despite his early apprehension, Bob quickly made a home for himself on television. Sponsors loved him for the way he flung himself wholeheartedly into carrying the product promotion through to the buying public. He never refused an interview, took the chance to plug his sponsor's name at every opportunity, did all kinds of promotions, made personal appearances and did a good job of cross-fertilization, publicizing his television shows with gags and direct plugs while on radio, in interviews and during his stage appearances. This 'added value' was worth thousands of dollars in publicizing the product — and to Bob himself in terms of his own good will with the sponsor. He sharpened the profile of his shows through his policy of top star guests and by doing what he had done in pictures: accepting the viewers' awareness of his presence, reputation and impact in other aspects of show business.

In the 1950s, for instance, he used *Roberta,* certainly one of his favourite shows, as the theme for a telecast, and on another occasion he featured clips from a dozen or so of his most famous films. The enormous success of his Christmas shows began in the 1950s, and in the 1960s a principal theme for one of his tele shows was his leading ladies, with a parade of beauties who included, of course, Dorothy Lamour. His versatility was extensive. He sang with Tom Jones, took a nostalgic look over his shoulder to his days in vaudeville with Jack Jones and Jimmy Durante, Petula Clark, Sammy Davis Jr and Juliet Prowse, and to the viewers' delight, gagged with Bing and danced and played classic sketches with the likes of Jack Benny.

His popularity as a television personality was not confined to his own shows. He made numerous guest appearances, was in greater demand than any other star as master of ceremonies for some of the most glittering occasions and hosted a number of 'telethons', the first of which took place in 1952 when, with Bing Crosby and Dorothy Lamour as co-hosts, he took on a unique

14½ hour telethon to raise a million dollars to send the 333-member US athletic team to Helsinki for the Olympic Games.

Even into the 1980s, when his television appearances for British audiences seemed to be restricted to fleeting tributes to others on *This is Your Life,* or when a Hollywood contemporary died, there was still that magical quality which Bob Hope, now into his eighties, seemed to project more than any other television personality when he came on screen. For close on twenty-five years he was the NBC network's topliner, a television superstar with an enormous following across the length and breadth of America. In what is perhaps the most fickle medium of all, he remained a constant star with a mass appeal which was as remarkable as it was extraordinary.

10 Bob 'The One and Only' Hope

Bob Hope over the years became an 'institution' with a private life exciting as much interest and speculation as his public life. That is not simply because of his great age (he was 99 on 29 May 2002) nor the fact that he is now retired from being a professional entertainer. Even at the peak of his career, when he was the biggest draw on radio and could name his own price for television and personal appearances, the public were always as fascinated by his family life, the money he was worth, the homes he lived in, the company he kept and the business deals he was negotiating as they were by his next movie part, stage appearance, radio spot or television series.

There was a fleeting moment at the very beginning when some people wondered if Bob's character-assassination of friend Crosby could really be as innocent as it was made out to be. Speculation about his relationship with Dolores punctured the surface from time to time, and when news stories tended to run thin, it was always fair game for the papers and 'human interest' magazines to ponder once more about just how much he was worth.

Typically, Bob Hope has tended to keep them guessing, dropping a hint here and quoting a figure there, but on the whole playing the part of the established pro and leaving them wanting more.

There is no doubt that he is extremely wealthy. Exactly how much he is worth he probably doesn't know himself to a couple of million dollars or so. In the early 1970s calculated guesses were running as high as $150 million. *Time* magazine went as high as $500 million, which reportedly prompted him to wire the editor with the message: 'If you can find it, we'll split it.' He typically milked the incident, telling troops in Saigon: 'If I had that kind of money I wouldn't come to Vietnam — I'd send for it.'

What is certain is that in 1940 alone he grossed almost $465,000 from radio, movies and personal appearances. As early as 1948 he was reliably reported to be making $150,000 a picture, and some of his later *Road* pictures, after seat prices had gone up, grossed $4½ million. In 1972 *Show* magazine reckoned he was probably the wealthiest man in show business, estimating his total assets at somewhere between $400 and $700 million. Bob would cunningly switch subjects when those sorts of figures were mentioned, after planting the seed that they were unlikely to be true anyway, but he reportedly admitted in the same interview that since 1954 he had never earned less than $1 million a year; and it is a matter of record that he once turned down a fee of $250,000 for a week at Las Vegas.

He grudgingly conceded in 1980 that: 'With my three houses and everything, I suppose I'm worth about $15 million.' But that wasn't counting some 10,000 acres of prime land in the San Fernando Valley and a Los Angeles suburb, where property values were even then at an astronomic level. At one time he was paying $1 million a year in state property tax and was forced to do a deal with the authorities and sell off some of his assets. More than fifty years ago his newspaper column alone was bringing him a tidy $30,000 a year and his earnings in 1946 topped $1.25 million. By this time astute advisers had already directed him into Government bonds and blue chip investment.

Most of his business and investment deals, though not all, have been profitable. One exception was a joint venture with Crosby in a new soft-drink called Lime Cola. Tempted by the promise of a large slice of the massive Coca-Cola market, Bob and Bing were each persuaded to put $25,000 into the enterprise. This goes back to the making of *Road to Rio* in 1947, when with a typical eye to the main chance, they decided to promote the product in the picture craftily by having a large sign displayed in the background of one of the scenes. Paramount's attorney Jack Karp argued that it wasn't possible, since that would constitute blatant advertising, but this was the first movie in which Crosby and Hope each had a one-third stake, and they put their two-thirds together and overruled the Paramount objection. The sign appeared in the film, and there it remained to cause embarrassment to the partners when the film continued to be screened long after Lime Cola had faded away and gone out of business, taking Bob's $25,000 with it.

It was a slightly earlier joint deal with Crosby which had inspired Hope to speculate when the Lime Cola opportunity came along. The two had become interested in a few thousand acres of land in Texas which was said to be good oil-prospecting country. They each put up $50,000, but when the drilling struck nothing but water, Bob was ready to call it a day and put it down to experience. Bing said he would put in another $50,000 if Bob would, and, reluctantly, he finally agreed. Just a few miles away from their original site the drillers hit the real stuff, with a find which promised to make them close to $3½ million each. Many years later Bob admitted that he made $4 million out of the oil strike and, taking skilful advice from an investment professional, turned some of that in for land and property.

He says that the acreage he bought in San Fernando Valley turned out to be gold. Vast tracts of land in California, Arizona and Nevada brought rich rewards. A lot of it was desert at the time, and friends told him he was crazy. But with houses and shopping centres now built on much of it, his income from this source has been enormous. Not long ago he was reputed to be the biggest single private property owner in California, though he claimed that, in calculating his worth, it was wrong to count in property he hadn't sold. He appears uninterested in arriving at a definitive figure, or indeed in revealing it, but once he did grudgingly admit: 'When I do sell, I'm going to be worth a lot of money.'

Bob Hope enjoys his enormous success as a businessman, even though he genuinely might not know what his income is. At one time he was said to own a race track and radio station and have a large stake in a record company and baseball team. His extreme prosperity has not slackened his natural appetite for a good business deal, and his career has shown that, despite his enormous wealth, he will fight hard to wring every cent out of a situation.

Many of those with whom Bob has been associated on a professional basis will agree that he doesn't demonstrate quite the same flair when it comes to paying out fees and, despite his bank balance, will still drive a hard bargain. The attitude probably goes back to the hard times his family went through when he was a boy and to the occasion when, selling newspapers on a street corner, he didn't have change when regular customer, John D.

Rockefeller, the legendary millionaire, handed over the money. 'Pay me tomorrow,' said boy Hope. But Rockefeller refused to be trusted. 'Never give credit when you can get cash,' he advised.

In other ways Bob's generosity is outstanding, and the enormous wealth which has come in part from being an entertainer could have been multiplied many times over if he had been paid for all his performances. His work for charity is virtually incalculable, his generosity legendary. He once gave a million dollars to a Texas university, $100,000 to build a church in Formosa. It is said that his Moorpark home and grounds, now worth millions of dollars, are donated to the Catholic church.

It is not surprising that Bob doesn't enjoy the speculation and occasional journalistic probings into his wealth. He once said that the only people who resent the money he has are journalists. Audiences are less envious, and in any event his wit and jokes about all the money he has, and how much he has to pay in tax, tend to take the sting out of any latent antagonism there might be. 'I need money,' he once announced in some kind of retort to the questioning, 'with a staff of thirty and those houses, never mind the government to support.'

Those houses have come in for a fair amount of exposure over the years. Not that Bob has been in them all that much. More of his life has been spent on the road, in theatres, on war-time concert stages, in television and film studios, doing personal appearances and charity appeals — even on aeroplanes and golf courses, than at home. Little wonder that the home he had built in Palm Springs, whose giant circular roof covers 25,000 square feet with a skylight sixty feet wide in the middle, raised a few eyebrows when it was being built. It cost $3 million and when the project was taking shape, one newspaper claimed it was bigger than the local department store. How could he justify expenditure of that magnitude when he already had other homes? Does he need to?

Bob looks back on the experience of building his Palm Springs home with mixed feelings. The problems seemed to be endless. The project stretched over nine long years, beset by disaster and controversy. The structure was half way up when a fire, said to be from a welder's spark, stopped everything. There were difficulties with the insurance cover, and he sued, finally agreeing to an out-of-court settlement.

The worst was to come when an old friend, Arthur Elrod, who had given him the original idea for the magnificent round house, was killed in a car crash. For a time the Hopes didn't have the heart to carry on, and the house was left there, abandoned, until local people began to fidget about what was going to happen to it. Bob and Dolores contemplated selling, but then decided to go ahead and finish it. 'I'm very glad we did,' said Bob, even though he adds, grinning, 'Pilots call it TWA West.'

The Hopes' Palm Springs home has many impressive and striking features, including a large indoor garden with its own waterfall, a restaurant-sized kitchen, exercise and leisure rooms, a dining-room which seats twenty in comfort, and an enormous living-room, topped by a hood which soars thirty feet high into the curved roof. There are individual bedroom areas, guest suites and superb grounds giving magnificent views of Palm Springs and the surrounding mountains. And predictably there is also a small golf course. Of two swimming pools, one is said to be the size of a small lake.

Since the 1930s, when the Hopes first settled to the idea of Bob's developing career being pivoted on pictures, they have had a base in Hollywood. When they first moved there from New York, they leased a house from Rhea Gable, wife of 1930s movie idol Clark, but once they fixed on a permanent move to the West Coast they rented an unfurnished house in Navajo Street in the Toluca Lake area of North Hollywood and had their furniture transported over from New York. The house was close to Lakeside, Bob's favourite golf course, and within easy travelling distance of the main film studios. Among the big stars who were their neighbours in those days were Crosby, W.C. Fields, Cagney and Bogart. Although Bob's Palm Springs house, just a twenty-minute commuter hop away by air, is infinitely more impressive, his Hollywood house has always been affectionately considered by the Hopes as their 'family home'.

In the first ten months after completion of the Palm Springs house, Bob managed to spend just four weeks there, so intensive was his schedule. It is his constant activity, which has taken him away from home and family for long and frequent periods, that not unnaturally has raised mild speculation from time to time about his marriage. Statistically, it is a model. The couple have now been together for seventy years, an astonishing record and almost unheard-of in the celluloid world of pictures.

But there can be little doubt that Bob's many absences over most of that time have placed an unusually heavy strain on the marriage. After her own marriage had ended in divorce, their then forty-year-old elder daughter Linda said in an interview in 1979: 'As a child I sensed things were not always going as well as one wanted them to. It may be presumptuous of me to say it, but I know there were times when the marriage was in danger.' Linda suggests that it was perhaps Dolores' devotion to the Roman Catholic faith that held the marriage together through difficult periods.

In the 1950s, when Bob's vagabond instincts were taking him away from home more than previously, it was suggested by some sharp-eyed columnists that Dolores was spending an unusual amount of time in the company of Roman Catholic churchmen — seeking counsel perhaps? There was speculation about an affair between Bob and the beautiful blonde actress Marilyn Maxwell, though nothing more than the sort of gossip likely to surround someone of his prominence who finds himself working with a beautiful girl in a number of pictures and on tour.

Bob's cavalier comment that he was 'no angel', whether accurate or not, tended for a while to fuel rumours at a time when *Confidential* magazine did a feature which pointed to an alleged affair with Barbara Payton, described later as a 'sexually active and publicity-seeking blonde starlet'. Whatever the facts, two certainties emerge: his reputation with his fans and the public was not harmed by the rumours and speculation; and his marriage has endured, even strengthened perhaps by the passing years, for Dolores' image has for a long time now been that of dutiful, understanding, supportive and loving wife. The strength of her attitude and her acceptance of Bob's love of travel emerge from comments she gave to author William Robert Faith in his book *Bob Hope, A Life in Comedy*, in which she said she had made a kind of peace with herself about his absences. 'He's done this all his life and has always travelled. I think he really loves that life,' she said. 'He's a rover by nature. The first year we were married I saw so little of Bob that I wasn't sure we'd make a go of it. Now, of course, I've gotten accustomed to his being away and couldn't imagine life being any different.'

From quite early on in Bob's career the strain of such a schedule with long stretches away from home, has also raised concern about his health. Overall though, he has remained astonishingly fit. When somebody raised the question with his brother Jack way back in the early war years, he retorted: 'Our grandfather still rides his bicycle to the pub at ninety-nine and Aunt Polly lived to be 103. We're a sturdy stock.' But Dolores once admitted that she never stopped worrying about Bob's health or his work overload. He sidesteps these notions with the comment that he takes good care of himself, which is true. He gave up smoking a long time ago, and drinks with extreme moderation. He is said to continue to exercise gently and, certainly in earlier years, was massaged regularly and liked to enjoy eight hours of sleep a night.

Celebrating his eightieth birthday in 1983, Bob said: 'People wonder why I work so hard. It's not work. I love what I'm doing. The greatest thing in the world is laughs. Laughs are excitement.' But with that disarming smile he did also admit: 'I'm slowing down a bit now, but I still need the laughs and the adulation.'

There have been times, as one would expect in a life now stretching towards its one hundredth year, when health problems have caused concern, by far the most serious being the recurring eye haemorrhaging which has required four operations.

The problem started in 1959 when dizzy spells persisted, brought on by what Bob self-diagnosed as exhaustion. He was on one of his famous overseas trips at the time, entertaining at an airforce base near Frankfurt, Germany, when he felt ill at an after-show party organized by the commanding officer. On the last stage of the trip, after a dance routine at a show in Iceland, he became dizzy again, and Dolores had a doctor's appointment arranged for him by the time he arrived home, early in the New Year. His blood pressure was high and he was warned to slow down. Later there were other incidents on the golf course, when he again felt dizzy and ill and his vision blurred — especially then when he stumbled and felt dizzy in the locker room. An eye specialist he consulted a few days later diagnosed a blood clot in the vein of his left cornea.

Bob half ignored warnings to ease up and continued with most of his commitments until his vision clouded to such an extent that he felt obliged to seek the advice of one of America's leading eye specialists. He was ready now to take notice, not daring to run the risk of losing his sight completely. He cancelled all engagements except his television show.

There was a brief return of the trouble the next year when Bob was making a USO trip to Alaska, and the dizziness returned while he was playing golf in Palm Springs in 1963. He sensed the haemorrhaging had started again and this time it was serious.

Agonizingly, Bob was compelled to spend three weeks in absolute quiet, some of the time in a darkened room. Two delicate operations were performed in quick succession, but he was determined to make his 1963 Bob Hope USO Christmas tour of Europe. The team flew out without him, but remarkably he joined them a few days later.

There was a recurrence of the problem in 1970, when Bob spent three days in the Jules Stein Eye Clinic. The trouble meant he had to cancel more dates. A couple of months later the familiar tell-tale dizziness was the prelude to another operation and five days' hospitalization in New York. In more recent years, though, his condition seems to have stabilized.

Despite Bob's obsession to perform and be almost constantly on the move, which has meant spending more of life away from his children and his wife than with them, he has a devout sense of family. This was apparent in the burgeoning days of his career when being one of seven brothers meant a lot to him. He made special efforts to keep in touch with them all after winning fame in Hollywood, always keen to neutralize any feeling that he was in some way special among them because he was an international celebrity.

One of Bob's fondest memories is of the monster family party he arranged in 1973, when he invited every living member of the Hope family to Los Angeles at his expense. They came from all over. The children alone numbered fifty.

Brother Jack became his business manager in 1938. He had ambitions to write songs with an eye to a career on the fringe of show business, but when Bob invited him to join the team, Jack didn't need a second invitation. In the 1940s Bob went into part-ownership with brother Ivor in a company called Hope Metal Products which immediately flourished and made them both useful sums of money.

His deep family feelings, which extended back to the love and affection he always had for his parents — whose fond memories he still cherishes, were wounded when two of his brothers, Sid and George, contracted cancer and died within a week of each other. George was fifty-eight, Sid just forty-one.

A bitter quarrel he had with brother Jim's wife, Marie, was emotionally bruising. The problem, which flared into a court battle in 1943, was about Bob's hiring Marie, at Jim's request, back in 1939. Bob was by then emerging as a major star earning big money, and Marie was taken on to help his secretary, Annabelle Pickett, with certain administrative duties and to handle specific things such as cataloguing his vast store of jokes and organizing his mailing of some eight thousand Christmas cards every year. It was agreed Marie be paid $50 a month for her few hours of evening work, but when she and Jim discovered how much Bob was earning, she felt she ought to be paid more. She said Bob agreed he would pay her a bonus, which was denied by his lawyers in court, and he is said to have countered by reminding her that he expected a $1,400 loan he had made to Jim to be paid back. Marie wanted back pay based on $50 dollars a week, not a month, and against Jim's wishes filed a $2,300 law suit when Bob didn't respond. Bob contested. The papers had a field day, though in the end perhaps rough justice was seen to have been done when the case was thrown out of court after the jury couldn't agree on a verdict.

Bob's children talk about him devotedly. He and Dolores were quite strict with them in their younger days and were keen to ensure that they didn't take for granted any privileges they might enjoy because of their parents' wealth. Standards of behaviour in his children were always important to Bob. None has followed him into the sharp end of show business, but though this doesn't seem to bother him, he did admit that he got a kick out of having Linda and Tony, his older children, work with him for a time, Linda on television specials and Tony as an assistant director on his tours.

Linda moved into the executive and creative side of Hope Enterprises, after being a school teacher, and despite suspicions of nepotism became vice-president on merit. She said: 'I've had to prove myself in this job, to cope with resentment to establish my credibility.' She has happy memories of growing up. 'Both my parents came from poor backgrounds and they kept a lot of the values they had when they were growing up and passed them on to us. We never had any fancy cars or all the luxuries that other show business people have.'

Linda remembers too how their parents, mainly Dolores, handled the adoption problem. 'We always knew we were adopted,' she revealed to a reporter once. 'My mother handled it really beautifully. I think I remember from the time I was small that we always used to pray for our natural mothers. There was never a sudden moment of revelation. It was always handled very much as being part of our lives.'

Linda insists that, although there were many times when they missed their father when they were growing up, during the times he made movies it wasn't as bad as many observers might have believed. 'When he was making a picture, we'd all have breakfast together and he would be just wonderful. He would read us little bits of script, talk to us about school and then, as he was leaving for the studio, he would always do a little tap dance or soft-shoe shuffle outside the window,' she said.

It was an extravagant occasion when Linda Theresa Roberta Hope married Nathaniel Greenblatt Lande at three o'clock on Saturday 11 January 1969 at St Charles Borromeo church, 10,828 Moorpark Street, North Hollywood. There were over a thousand guests to enjoy a spectacular reception on the back lawns of the Hope mansion, where a gigantic white silk tent was the centrepiece of the celebrations. Top brass from Washington and the armed services were there, including Vice-President elect Spiro Agnew (substituting for Richard Nixon) and Ronald Reagan, then Governor of California, and Nancy, along with scores of well-known personalities from the world of pictures and the media, including Dotty Lamour and her husband, Bill Howard, and Bing and Kathryn Crosby. It was a proud occasion for Hope and a chance for the appropriate joke: 'When she was young I was away so much she rarely saw me. When she did, she thought I was the gas-meter man trying to get fresh with her mother,' he quipped. By comparison, when Nora married, she wanted a much quieter affair. There was a lump the size of a tennis ball in Bob's throat when she turned to him afterwards and said: 'I've always been so proud that I have a father everybody loves.'

The four adopted children, now all adult of course, get on well together, though in earlier years they did not see one another very often because they were spread about the country so much: Linda was in Hollywood, working out of the Hope Company building not far from the family home at Toluca Lake; Anthony got married, had two children and worked as an attorney in Washington; Nora, whose daughter is now an adult, divorced, remarried and went to live near San Francisco, and the remaining member of the Hope clan, Kelly, also went to live in San Francisco to work in a science museum.

Bob must surely be the world's best loved entertainer. The hundreds of benefits and charity appearances he has made over the years have raised billions of dollars for deserving causes, and he has been honoured also as a performer, an artist, and a radio, television and film celebrity without equal. His style, professionalism and ability to relate to an audience have been universally admired, and his glibness and slightly jaunty arrogance have been balanced by an underlying sincerity which has made him everybody's friend.

In the country he adopted one would expect him to have won such honours as Leading Entertainer and Leading Comedian awards, the Congressional Medal of Honor, Best Male Performer award, even the Comedian of the Century award and the Distinguished Service Medal, but in the country of his birth, less generous in the doling out of honours, a distinction which Hope particularly treasures is the Honorary Order of the British Empire, conferred on him on 1 July 1976 at the British Embassy in Washington. In making the presentation, the British Ambassador, Sir Peter Ramsbotham, said that Bob was regarded with enormous affection in Britain and that he was known to be a favourite of the royal family.

Bob has scores of honorary degrees and has had buildings named after him, most recently a new cultural centre at Palm Desert, California. On an unprecedented occasion, America's House of Representatives stopped their normal business to pay tribute to him, as the keynote of an extraordinary two-day national tribute on his seventy-fifth birthday. To mark the occasion the USO decided to name their new headquarters in Washington 'The Bob Hope USO Center', in recognition of all he had done for the armed forces. Then there was a huge family party attended by more than two hundred 'close friends and family'. The following day he was summoned to attend the House of Representatives, where normal business was suspended for a full hour while official tributes were made. Speaker after speaker honoured him — for the countless hours he had given to serve his country and worthy charities; for his humour; for his devotion and loyalty to Americans and America; for spending Christmas in selfless devotion to others in the heat of Vietnam and the cold of Germany when he could have been comfortable at home with his family; and, as one speaker remarked, for lightening the hearts, faces and spirits of thousands of servicemen and women.

For Bob it was one of the most moving and emotional moments of his life. Dolores, Linda, Nora, Tony, Kelly, four grandchildren and his one surviving brother, Fred, accompanied him into the VIP seats in the gallery of the House of Representatives. This remarkable occasion ended when Speaker 'Tip' O'Neill said Bob was a fine American and a great American, and the whole house sang 'Happy Birthday' and cheered and clapped enthusiastically. Bob's eyes were tearful as he acknowledged the honour, his family standing by his side joining in.

Once or twice during his long career Bob Hope hinted at the possibility of retirement, but at the same time kept up his hyperactivity so that nobody, least of all himself, has taken the comments seriously. You could now refer to him as having effectively retired, though he wouldn't thank you for it. Many years ago, when he was seventy-six, he said: 'Laughter is the only tonic I need to keep young. Right now I feel good, though sometimes I have to pace myself a little.' That was in deference to a minor heart disturbance he had the previous year after he had pushed himself hard through four hours of tap dancing. 'I just worked too hard and the tempo of my heart speeded up,' he said. In 1976 he reckoned he worked 261 out of the 366 days.

So much has Bob become part of the American way of life that he was once described as an extra star on the American flag. In 1983, just before his birthday, he declared: 'I don't believe I'll be eighty. I think there's a mistake.' What has kept him going for so long is his deep-down, almost instinctive urge to perform and entertain. When ordered by his doctor to take it easy for a while by going on a month's sea cruise, he was back in Los Angeles in a week. When his doctor asked the reason for his quick return, he responded simply: 'Fish don't applaud.' The comment perhaps said more about his back-breaking professional life-style than he imagined. He has so enjoyed it all that it is impossible to imagine his ever retiring officially.

Bob has responded to almost all situations and occasions, disappointments and major triumphs with that supreme air of professionalism and of course with a gag. He is casual, gentler in manner than you might imagine, courteous in private life, and makes no secret that he has relished the adulation and the honours which have come his way, while accepting them with an almost distant, if enthusiastic, dignity. The respect he has earned from ordinary individuals has also meant much to him.

In 1991, the then 88 years old Bob Hope, with his wife Dolores, was again in the UK and received an enormous welcome from the residents of Eltham in south-east London. He had given almost £60,000 towards the renovation of the Eltham Little Theatre which had been facing closure as far back as 1978 and, in addition, had donated the proceeds from a sell-out show at the London Palladium, his first West End appearance in seven years. Outside the famous theatre Bob was thrilled to have a special word with Mrs Florence Ching, who since 1942 had lived in the house where he was born.

Despite his advanced age, Hope, along with Dolores and their 21-year-old grandson Zachary, made time to visit relatives and friends in Hertfordshire, spending over an hour chatting with his first cousin Frank Symonds, before taking twenty-four of his English relatives to a celebration meal at a nearby hotel.

Asked at that time if he planned to go on working for ever, Bob replied: 'Well ... I have so far and for as long as I feel good.' In June 2000, when 97 years old, that resolve was critically in doubt when he received emergency treatment for an intestinal problem. His condition at that time was considered to be so serious that his family asked people to pray for his recovery.

Recover he did, of course, and was thus able to continue to enjoy the respect and affection of a huge public worldwide who have no doubt whatsoever that Bob Hope will go down in history as one of the greatest-ever 'wise-crackers' in the business.

The Joke Factory

Bob Hope is a man in a million, in more ways than one. He is a multi-millionaire, has travelled more than a million miles to entertain the American armed forces and has a million personal jokes, all listed, coded and catalogued. He hired his first gag-writer, Al Boasberg, in 1929 and started a trend. He is known to millions of fans for his jokes. Here is just a small sample from them, as he might well introduce himself: 'This is Bob (man of a million one-liners) Hope.'

About England
Every time I stay in one of those grand old English hotels, I expect Shakespeare to bring up the towels.

On Crosby's wealth
They operated on him for gallstones and found uranium.

About jogging on his seventy-fifth birthday
No. I don't want to jog because I don't want to have to hire a nurse to follow me.

About his happy marriage
We have been married forty-five years, and I have been home three weeks. It makes it very interesting when you come home and have to be introduced to the children.

When he made a return visit to the house where he was born in Eltham
I'm trying to remember if I owe any rent.

About his continued working
I go on working because I have a government to support.

About going into hospital
When I first went to hospital I chased the nurses. Now I look for a wheel-chair so that I can chase the nurses.

On dying
When I die they'd better nail the lid of the box down pretty quick — or I'll be up right away for an encore.

About Reagan running for President
Boy, I hope he makes it this time because his hair can't stay that colour forever.

On President Carter
He used to worry about being a one-term President. Now he's worried whether they'll count this one.

Of his earlier boxing as a semi-pro
I used to fight under the name of Rembrandt Hope I was on the canvas so much. I was a colourful fighter — I wore blue trunks with a yellow streak down my back.

About England
I like England. Here the girls whistle back at you.

About himself
I'm such a ham. Somebody said that, if I were in a blizzard and two Eskimo dogs walked by, I'd do ten minutes for them.

About his jokes
My brother writes my jokes. Some day I'm going up into the attic and loosen his strait-jacket.

On his absence from home
I'm away from home so much my wife has our towels marked 'Hers' and 'Welcome Stranger'.

On the Russians
I don't think it was a good idea to restrict Khrushchev to his hotel while he was in New York . . . I think they should have let him take his chances in traffic like the rest of us.

About his film career
I was going to play the title role in *The Love Machine,* but Ralph Nader had me recalled to the factory for faulty parts.

About Phyllis Diller
We had to pay Phyllis a lot of money for the picture. She needed it. Her make-up man got stunt pay.

About his film Paris Holiday
I always wanted to produce a picture with a message. I got my
way with *Paris Holiday*. The message: 'Stick to acting.'

On his own birth
Call a doctor. There's been a terrible mistake. They've taken the
baby and left the stork.

On the title of the Road *pictures*
You know why they were called *Road* pictures? Because Dotty
Lamour was always giving us the Stop sign.

On Billy Graham's golf
It's hard to beat a guy who gets a ball out of a sand trap just by
muttering a few words and looking up.

On Perry Como's golf
One day we were all complimenting Perry about keeping his
head down until we realized he'd fallen asleep.

Postscript
He has made fifty-five movies, done 300 television shows and
spent twelve years fronting a weekly radio show. There were
scores of overseas tours and he has written seven books.

Franklin Roosevelt set something of a routine when he
became the first US President to invite Bob Hope to the White
House, and there would be no Eisenhower Memorial Hospital
had Bob not raised $10 million.

He is an Honorary Commander of the British Empire and has
met most members of the royal family.

Some forty-plus years ago, in a radio poll, around eighty per
cent of those who responded said they would vote for him as
President.

Feature Films Listing

Bob Hope began making films in 1934 while in New York and made his first feature film in Hollywood in 1937. That was *The Big Broadcast of 1938*, released by Paramount on 18 February 1938. Between 1938 and 1972 he made fifty-four feature films. The first *Road* film was *Road to Singapore* released in 1940. Altogether there were seven *Road* films released in this order: *Singapore* (1940), *Zanzibar* (1941), *Morocco* (1942), *Utopia* (1945), *Rio* (1947), *Bali* (1952) and *Hong Kong* (1962).

There were also two mini-series with different co-stars. With Paulette Goddard he was featured in *The Cat and the Canary, The Ghost Breakers* and *Nothing but the Truth*. In the *My Favourite Spy* series he starred with Madeleine Carroll (*My Favourite Blonde*), Dorothy Lamour (*My Favourite Brunette*) and Hedy Lamarr (*My Favourite Spy*). Shirley Ross, who shared his first major triumph in *The Big Broadcast of 1938*, was also with him in *Thanks for the Memory* and *Some Like It Hot*. In *The Paleface* and *Son of Paleface* he starred with Jane Russell.

Bob's short comedies, released in 1934, 1935 and 1936, were *Going Spanish* (Educational Films) with Leah Ray; *Paree, Paree* (Warner Brothers) with Dorothy Stone; *The Old Grey Mayor* (Warner Brothers) with Ruth Blasco; *Watch the Birdie* (Warner Brothers) with Neil O'Day; *Double Exposure* (Warner Brothers) with Jules Epailley; *Calling All Tars* (Warner Brothers) with Johnny Berkes; and *Shop Talk* (Warner Brothers). He also made a number of short movies in which he appeared as himself, including *Don't Hook Now*, about the Bing Crosby golf tournament (1938), *Welcome to Britain*, as a behaviour guide to American soldiers serving in wartime Britain (1943), *The Heart of Show Business*, about the Variety Clubs (1957) and *Hollywood Star-Spangled Revue*, promoting US Treasury bonds (1966).

The Big Broadcast of 1938   1938
Paramount
Producer: Harlan Thompson

Director: Mitchell Leisen
Appeared with W.C. Fields, Martha Raye, Dorothy Lamour,
  Shirley Ross, Lynne Overman, Ben Blue and Leif Erickson.
Songs included 'Thanks for the Memory' (Academy Award
  Winner) and 'You Took the Words Right Out of My
  Heart'.

College Swing (GB: Swing, Teacher Swing)   1938
Paramount
Producer: Lewis Gensler
Director: Raoul Walsh
Appeared with George Burns, Gracie Allen, Martha Raye,
  Edward Everett Horton, Florence George, Ben Blue, Betty
  Grable, Jackie Coogan, John Payne, Robert Cummings,
  Skinnay Ennis and Jerry Colonna.
Songs included 'I Fall in Love With You Every Day'

Give Me a Sailor   1938
Paramount
Producer: Jeff Lazarus
Director: Elliott Nugent
Appeared with Martha Raye and Betty Grable.
Songs included 'What Goes On Here in My Heart?' and 'A
  Little Kiss at Twilight'.

Thanks for the Memory   1938
Paramount
Director: George Archainbaud
Associate Producer: Mel Shauer
Appeared with Shirley Ross, Charles Butterworth, Otto
  Kruger, Hedda Hopper and Patricia Wilder.
Songs included 'Thanks for the Memory' and 'Two Sleepy
  People'.

Never Say Die   1939
Paramount
Producer: Paul Jones
Director: Elliott Nugent
Appeared with Martha Raye, Andy Devine, Alan Mowbray,
  Gale Sondergaard and Monty Woolley.
Songs included 'The Tra La La and the Oom Pah Pah'.

Some Like It Hot 1939
Paramount
Associate Producer: William C. Thomas
Director: George Archainbaud
Appeared with Shirley Ross, Una Merkel, Gene Krupa, Rufe
  Davis, Bernard Nedell, Frank Sully, Bernadene Hayes and
  Richard Denning.
Songs included 'The Lady's in Love with You' and 'Some
  Like It Hot'.

The Cat and the Canary 1939
Paramount
Producer: Arthur Hornblow Jr
Director: Elliott Nugent
Appeared with Paulette Goddard, John Beal, Douglass
  Montgomery, Gale Sondergaard and Elizabeth Patterson.

Road to Singapore 1940
Paramount
Producer: Harlan Thompson
Director: Victor Schertzinger
Appeared with Bing Crosby, Dorothy Lamour, Charles
  Coburn, Judith Barrett, Anthony Quinn, Jerry Colonna,
  Johnny Arthur, Pierre Watkin, Gaylord Pendleton, Miles
  Mander and Pedro Regas.
Songs included 'Too Romantic', 'Sweet Potato Piper',
  'Kaigoon' and 'The Moon and the Willow Tree'

The Ghost Breakers 1940
Paramount
Producer: Arthur Hornblow Jr
Director: George Marshall
Appeared with Paulette Goddard, Richard Carlson, Paul
  Lukas, Anthony Quinn, Willie Best, Pedro de Cordoba,
  Virginia Brissac, Noble Johnson, Tom Dugan, Paul Fix
  and Lloyd Corrigan.

Road to Zanzibar 1941
Paramount
Producer: Paul Jones
Director: Victor Schertzinger
Appeared with Bing Crosby, Dorothy Lamour, Una Merkel,

Eric Blore, Luis Alberni, Joan Marsh, Ethel Greer, Iris Adrian and Georges Renavent.
Songs included 'It's Always You', 'You're Dangerous', 'You Lucky People, You' and 'African Etude'.

Caught in the Draft 1941
Paramount
Producer: B.G. DeSylva
Director: David Butler
Appeared with Dorothy Lamour, Lynne Overman, Eddie Bracken, Clarence Kolb, Paul Hurst, Ferike Boros and Phyllis Ruth.

Nothing but the Truth 1941
Paramount
Producer: Arthur Hornblow Jr
Director: Elliott Nugent
Appeared with Paulette Goddard, Edward Arnold, Leif Erickson, Glenn Anders, Helen Vinson, Grant Mitchell, Willie Best, Clarence Kolb, Catherine Doucet, Mary Forbes, Rose Hobart, Leon Belasco and Helene Millard.

Louisiana Purchase 1941
Paramount
Associate Producer: Harold Wilson
Director: Irving Cummings
Appeared with Vera Zorina, Victor Moore, Irene Bordoni, Dona Drake, Raymond Walburn, Maxie Rosenbloom, Frank Albertson, Phyllis Ruth, Donald McBride, Andrew Tombes, Robert Warwick, Charles La Torre, Charles Lasky, Emory Parnell, Iris Meredith, Catherine Craig and Jack Norton.
Songs included 'Louisiana Purchase', 'You're Lonely and I'm Lonely' and 'It's a Lovely Day Tomorrow'.

My Favourite Blonde 1942
Paramount
Associate Producer: Paul Jones
Director: Sidney Lanfield
Appeared with Madeleine Carroll, Gale Sondergaard, George Zucco, Victor Varconi, Lionel Royce and Crane Whitley.

Road to Morocco   1942
Paramount
Associate Producer: Paul Jones
Director: David Butler
Appeared with Bing Crosby, Dorothy Lamour, Anthony
    Quinn, Dona Drake, Vladimir Sokoloff, Mikhail
    Rasumny, Jamiel Hanson, Monte Blue, Louise La
    Planche, Theo de Voe, Brooke Evans, Suzanne Ridgeway,
    Patsy Mace and Yvonne de Carlo.
Songs included 'Moonlight Becomes You'.

Star-Spangled Rhythm   1942
Paramount
Associate Producer: Joseph Sistrom
Director: George Marshall
Appeared with Bing Crosby, Ray Milland, Vera Zorina,
    Eddie Bracken, Victor Moore, Mary Martin, Veronica
    Lake, Fred MacMurray, Dorothy Lamour, Dick Powell,
    Alan Ladd, Franchot Tone, Paulette Goddard, Betty
    Hutton, Rochester, William Bendix, Susan Hayward,
    Lynne Overman, Cass Daley, Walter Catlett, Jerry
    Colonna, Marjorie Reynolds, Gary Crosby, Ernest Truex,
    Sterling Holloway, Macdonald Carey, Betty Rhodes,
    Johnny Johnston, Katherine Dunham, Walter Abel, Dona
    Drake, Gil Lamb, Arthur Treacher, Cecil B. De Mille,
    Preston Sturges, Ralph Murphy, Anne Revere, Edward
    Fielding, Edgar Dearing, William Haade, Maynard
    Holmes, James Millican, Eddie Johnson, Slim and Slam,
    Walter Wahl, Golden Gate Quartette.
Songs included 'That Old Black Magic' and 'Let's Hit the
    Road to Dreamland'.

They Got Me Covered   1943
RKO Radio
Producer: Samuel Goldwyn
Director: David Butler
Appeared with Dorothy Lamour, Lenore Aubert, Otto
    Preminger, Eduardo Ciannelli, Marion Martin, Donald
    Meek, Phyllis Ruth, Philip Ahn, Donald McBride, Mary
    Treen, Bettye Avery, Margaret Hayes, Mary Byrne,

William Tetter, Henry Guttman, Florence Bates and
Walter Catlett.

Let's Face It   1943
Paramount
Associate Producer: Fred Kohlmar
Director: Sidney Lanfield
Appeared with Betty Hutton, ZaSu Pitts, Phyllis Povah, Dave
   Willock, Eve Arden, Cully Richards, Marjorie Weaver,
   Dona Drake, Raymond Walburn, Andrew Tombes, Arthur
   Loft, Joe Sawyer, Grace Hayle, Evelyn Dockson, Andria
   Moreland, Kay Linaker and Brooke Evans.
Songs included 'Let's Not Talk about Love'.

The Princess and the Pirate   1944
RKO Radio
Producer: Samuel Goldwyn
Director: David Butler
Appeared with Virginia Mayo, Walter Brennan, Walter
   Slezak and Victor McLaglen.
Songs included 'Kiss Me in the Moonlight'.

Road to Utopia   1945
Paramount
Producer: Paul Jones
Director: Hal Walker
Appeared with Bing Crosby, Dorothy Lamour, Hillary
   Brooke, Douglass Dumbrille, Jack La Rue, Robert Barrat,
   Nestor Paiva, Robert Benchley, Will Wright and Jimmy
   Dundee.
Songs included 'Would You' and 'Anybody's Dream'.

Monsieur Beaucaire   1946
Paramount
Producer: Paul Jones
Director: George Marshall
Appeared with Joan Caulfield, Patric Knowles, Marjorie
   Reynolds, Cecil Kellaway, Joseph Schildkraut, Reginald
   Owen, Constance Collier and Hillary Brooke.

My Favourite Brunette   1947
Paramount
Producer: Daniel Dare
Director: Elliott Nugent
Appeared with Dorothy Lamour, Peter Lorre, Lon Chaney,
   John Hoyt, Charles Dingle, Reginald Denny, Frank
   Puglia, Ann Doran, Willard Robertson and Jack La Rue.

Variety Girl   1947
Paramount
Producer: Daniel Dare
Director: George Marshall
   Appeared with Mary Hatcher, Olga San Juan, DeForest
   Kelley, William Demarest, Frank Faylen and Frank
   Ferguson.

Where There's Life   1947
Paramount
Producer: Paul Jones
Director: Sidney Lanfield
Appeared with Signe Hasso, William Bendix, George
   Coulouris, Vera Marshe, George Zucco, Dennis Hoey and
   John Alexander.

Road to Rio   1947
Paramount
Producer: Daniel Dare
Director: Norman Z. McLeod
Appeared with Bing Crosby, Dorothy Lamour, Gale
   Sondergaard, Frank Faylen, Joseph Vitale, Frank Puglia,
   Nestor Paiva, Robert Barrat, Jerry Colonna, the Wiere
   Brothers and the Andrews Sisters.
Songs included 'But Beautiful', 'You Don't Have to Know
   the Language' and 'Experience'.

The Paleface   1948
Paramount
Producer: Robert L. Welch
Director: Norman Z. McLeod
Appeared with Jane Russell, Robert Armstrong, Iris

Adrian, Robert Watson, Jack Searl, Joseph Vitale, Charles
Trowbridge, Clem Bevans, Jeff York and Stanley Andrews.
Songs included: 'Buttons and Bows'.

Sorrowful Jones   1949
Paramount
Producer: Robert L. Welch
Director: Sidney Lanfield
Appeared with Lucille Ball, William Demarest, Bruce Cabot,
    Thomas Gomez, Tom Pedi, Paul Lees, Houseley
    Stevenson, Ben Weldon and Mary Jane Saunders.

The Great Lover   1949
Paramount
Producer: Edmund Beloin
Director: Alexander Hall
Appeared with Rhonda Fleming, Roland Young, Roland
    Culver, Richard Lyon, Gary Gray, Jerry Hunter and
    Jackie Jackson.

Fancy Pants   1950
Paramount
Producer: Robert L. Welch
Director: George Marshall
Appeared with Lucille Ball, Bruce Cabot, Jack Kirkwood,
    Lea Penman, Hugh French and Eric Blore.

The Lemon Drop Kid   1951
Paramount
Producer: Robert L. Welch
Director: Sidney Lanfield
Appeared with Marilyn Maxwell, Lloyd Nolan, Jane
    Darwell, Andrea King, Fred Clark, Jay C. Flippen and
    William Frawley.
Songs included 'It Doesn't Cost a Dime to Dream' and 'Silver
    Bells'.

My Favourite Spy   1951
Paramount
Producer: Paul Jones
Director: Norman Z. McLeod

Appeared with Hedy Lamarr, Francis L. Sullivan, Arnold
Moss, Tonio Selwart, Stephen Chase, John Archer and
Morris Ankrum.

Son of Paleface   1952
Paramount
Producer: Robert L. Welch
Director: Frank Tashlin
Appeared with: Jane Russell, Roy Rogers, Bill Williams,
Lloyd Corrigan, Paul E. Burns, Douglass Dumbrille and
Harry Von Zell.
Songs included 'Four-legged Friend' and 'Buttons and Bows'.

Road to Bali   1952
Paramount
Producer: Harry Tugend
Director: Hal Walker
Appeared with Bing Crosby, Dorothy Lamour, Murvyn Vye,
Peter Coe, Ralph Moody and Leon Askin
Songs included 'Chicago Style'.

Off Limits (GB: Military Policemen)   1953
Paramount
Producer: Harry Tugend
Director: George Marshall
Appeared with Mickey Rooney, Marilyn Maxwell, Eddie
Mayehoff, Stanley Clements, Jack Dempsey, Marvin
Miller and John Ridgely.
Songs included 'Military Policemen', 'All About Love'.

Here Come the Girls   1953
Paramount
Producer: Paul Jones
Director: Claude Binyon
Appeared with Arlene Dahl, Rosemary Clooney, Tony
Martin, Millard Mitchell, William Demarest, Fred Clark
and Robert Strauss.
Songs included 'Ya Got Class' and 'It's Torment'.

Casanova's Big Night   1954
Paramount

Producer: Paul Jones
Director: Norman Z. McLeod
Appeared with Joan Fontaine, Audrey Dalton, Basil
   Rathbone, Hugh Marlowe, Arnold Moss, John Carradine,
   John Hoyt, Hope Emerson, Robert Hutton, Lon Chaney
   Jr, Raymond Burr, Frieda Inescort and Primo Carnera.

The Seven Little Foys   1955
Paramount
Producer: Jack Rose
Director: Melville Shavelson
Appeared with Milly Vitale, Angela Clarke, George Tobias,
   Billy Gray, Leif Erickson, Paul de Rolf, Linda Bennett,
   Lydia Reed, Tommy Duran, Jimmy Baird and James
   Cagney
Songs include 'Mary's a Grand Old Name', 'Chinatown' and
   'Yankee Doodle Boy'

That Certain Feeling   1956
Paramount
Producer: Norman Panama and Melvin Frank
Director: Norman Panama
Appeared with Eva Marie Saint, George Sanders, Pearl
   Bailey, David Lewis, Al Capp, Jerry Mathers, Herbert
   Rudley and Florenz Ames.
Songs included 'That Certain Feeling', 'Hit the Road to
   Dreamland' and 'Zing! Went the Strings of My Heart'.

The Iron Petticoat   1956
Metro-Goldwyn-Mayer
Producer: Betty Box
Director: Ralph Thomas
Appeared with Katharine Hepburn, James Robertson Justice,
   Robert Helpmann, David Kossoff, Alan Gifford, Paul
   Carpenter, Noelle Middleton, Nicholas Phipps, Sidney
   James, Alexander Gauge, Doris Goddard, Tutte Lemkow,
   Sandra Dorne and Richard Wattis.

Beau James   1957
Paramount
Producer: Jack Rose

Director: Melville Shavelson
Appeared with Vera Miles, Paul Douglas, Alexis Smith,
   Darren McGavin, Joe Mantell, Horace MacMahon,
   Richard Shannon, Willis Bouchey, Sid Melton, George
   Jessel and Walter Catlett. Cameos: Jack Benny and Jimmy
   Durante.
Songs included 'Manhattan', and 'Sidewalks of New York'.

Paris Holiday   1958
United Artists
Producer: Bob Hope
Director: Gerd Oswald
Appeared with Fernandel, Anita Ekberg, Martha Hyer,
   Preston Sturges, André Morell, Alan Gifford, Maurice
   Teynac, Ives Brainville and Jean Murat

Alias Jesse James   1959
United Artists
Executive Producer: Bob Hope
Director: Norman Z. McLeod
Appeared with Rhonda Fleming, Wendell Corey, Jim Davis,
Will Wright and Mary Young.

The Facts of Life   1960
United Artists
Producer: Norman Panama
Director: Melvin Frank
Appeared with Lucille Ball, Ruth Hussey, Don DeFore,
   Louis Nye, Philip Ober, Marianne Stewart and Peter
   Leeds.

Bachelor in Paradise   1961
Metro-Goldwyn-Mayer
Producer: Ted Richmond
Director: Jack Arnold
Appeared with Lana Turner, Janis Paige, Jim Hutton, Paula
   Prentiss, Don Porter, Virginia Grey, Agnes Moorehead
   and Florence Sundstrom.

Road to Hong Kong   1962
United Artists

Producer: Melvin Frank
Director: Norman Panama
Appeared with Bing Crosby, Joan Collins, Dorothy Lamour,
   Robert Morley, Walter Gotell, Roger Delgado, Felix
   Aylmer, Peter Madden, Alan Gifford, Robert Ayres,
   Robin Hughes, Julian Sherrier, Bill Nagy, Guy Standeven,
   John McCarthy, Simon Levy, Jacqueline Jones, Victor
   Brooks, Roy Patrick, John Dearth and David Randall.
Cameo appearance of Jerry Colonna, David Niven, Peter
   Sellers, Dean Martin and Frank Sinatra.
Songs included 'Teamwork'.

Critic's Choice   1963
Warner Brothers
Producer: Frank P. Rosenberg
Director: Don Weis
Appeared with Lucille Ball, Marilyn Maxwell, Rip Torn,
   Jessie Royce Landis, John Dehner, Jim Backus, Ricky
   Kelman and Dorothy Green.

Call Me Bwana   1963
United Artists
Producer: Albert R. Broccoli
Director: Gordon Douglas
Appeared with Anita Ekberg, Edie Adams, Lionel Jeffries,
   Arnold Palmer, Percy Herbert, Paul Carpenter, Bari
   Jonson and Orlando Martins.

A Global Affair   1964
Metro-Goldwyn-Mayer
Producer: Hall Bartlett
Director: Jack Arnold
   Appeared with Lilo Pulver, Michèle Mercier, Elga Andersen,
   Yvonne De Carlo, Miiko Taka, Robert Sterling and
   Nehemiah Persoff.

I'll Take Sweden   1965
United Artists
Producer: Edward Small
Director: Frederick De Cordova
Appeared with Tuesday Weld, Frankie Avalon, Dina Merrill,
   Jeremy Slate, Rosemarie Frankland, Walter Sande, John

Qualen, Peter Bourne, Fay De Witt, Alice Frost and Roy Roberts.

Songs included 'I'll Take Sweden', 'Watusi Joe', 'The Bells Keep Ringing', 'Take It Off' and 'There'll Be Rainbows Again'.

Boy, Did I Get a Wrong Number! 1966
United Artists
Producer: Edward Small
Director: George Marshall
Appeared with Elke Sommer, Phyllis Diller, Cesare Danova, Marjorie Lord, Kelly Thorsdon, Benny Baker, Terry Burnham and Joyce Jameson.

Eight on the Lam (GB: Eight on the Run) 1967
United Artists
Associate Producer: Bill Lawrence
Director: George Marshall
Appeared with Phyllis Diller, Jonathan Winters, Shirley Eaton, Jill St. John, Stacey Maxwell, Kevin Brody, Robert Hope, Glenn Gilger, Avis Hope, Debi Storm, Michael Freeman, Austin Willis and Peter Leeds.

The Private Navy of Sergeant O'Farrell 1968
United Artists
Producer: John Beck
Director: Frank Tashlin
Appeared with Phyllis Diller, Jeffrey Hunter, Gina Lollobrigida, Mylene Demongeot, John Myhers, Mako, Henry Wilcoxon, Dick Sargent, Christopher Dark, Michael Burns, William Wellman Jr, Robert Donner, Jack Grinnage, William Christopher and John Spina.

How to Commit Marriage 1971
Cinerama
Producer: Bill Lawrence
Director: Norman Panama
Appeared with Jackie Gleason, Jane Wyman, Maureen Arthur, Leslie Nielsen, Tina Louise, Paul Stewart, Irwin Corey, Joanna Cameron and Tim Mathieson.

Cancel My Reservation   1972
Warner Brothers
Executive Producer: Bob Hope
Director: Paul Bogart
Appeared with Eva Marie Saint, Ralph Bellamy, Forrest
   Tucker, Keenan Wynn, Doodles Weaver, Betty Ann Carr,
   Henry Darrow, Chief Dan George, Anne Archer, Herb
   Vigran and Pat Morita.

Index